C000005942

Open Tribe

to an inspiration!

love

Sue

Open Tribe

Sue Goss

Lawrence & Wishart, London 2014

Lawrence and Wishart Limited
99a Wallis Road
London
E9 5LN

© Sue Goss 2014
Published in association with Compass

The author has asserted her rights under the Copyright, Design and Patents
Act, 1998 to be identified as the author of this work.

All rights reserved. Apart from fair dealing for the purpose of private study,
research, criticism or review, no part of this publication may be reproduced,
stored in a retrieval system, or transmitted, in any form or by any means,
electronic, electrical, chemical, mechanical, optical, photocopying, recording
or otherwise, without the prior permission of the copyright owner.

ISBN 9781909831100

British Library Cataloguing in Publication Data.
A catalogue record for this book is available from the British Library

Contents

Foreword Neal Lawson   7

Introduction   9

1. The open tribe   17
2. What are we like?   34
3. Why is politics so childish?   49
4. On the side of the people not the machine   67
5. Can the state love?   84
6. Change always starts at the edge   106
7. 'We are the 99%'   131

Conclusions   143
Biographies of main interviewees   158

FOREWORD: A POLITICS THAT IS MORE LIKE PEOPLE

This glorious book is about how we move towards a new way of doing politics.

In the twenty-first century, the politics of two classes, two parties and two global superpowers has shattered into a gyroscope of complexity. And yet little has changed in our political culture. Rather than being liberated by the possibilities of the times we now live in, party politics still tends to be top-down, centralised, based on command and control – and above all it tends to be closed. The assumption is that power resides in the state, and control over the levers of the state is everything.

Old ways of doing politics – binary, narrow, adversarial and tribal – are hindering our ability to innovate and experiment just when we most need it. Complex challenges – floods and financialisation, consumerisation and individualisation – demand equally complex and nuanced responses.

Meanwhile, there are many places where a different form of politics is really kicking in. People are meeting, talking, collaborating and sharing as never before.

Technology allows peer-to-peer and many-to-many networks to define new ways of thinking, acting and being that have openness at their cultural heart. Can you learn, adapt, relate and have empathy with those you need to work alongside in order to succeed? These are the traits that matter in these new times – and they apply to our public, private and civil lives.

And yet ... there is something about the notion of tribe that grips us. We want to belong, to be loyal, to believe and demonstrate solidarity. We are tribal creatures – it's deep in our DNA. There is here an abiding paradox, which this book seeks to unpick:

7

we need a shared identity with a group or tribe – 'our people' – but we also need to be open, to experiment, innovate and learn. A paradox of course cannot be solved – we merely have to learn how to live with its frustrating and endless tensions.

This is why the notion of the Open Tribe is so important. It gives us a frame, a way of understanding and being, which lets us belong but also lets us adapt and therefore survive and maybe even thrive. The open tribe has a core set of beliefs and values, but it will let itself be tested; it will talk to those with whom it doesn't agree. Not least because, as Gramsci said, 'there is always a grain of truth in your enemy's argument'. The Open Tribe doesn't want to 'win', but to learn, collaborate and build its networks. More than anything, the Open Tribe recognises that means cannot be divorced from ends – a good society cannot be created by doing bad things. So what matters is how the tribe behaves and whether it prefigures what it wants the good society to look and feel like. The journey is all.

The challenge that Sue Goss sets out here is a simple one: can we make a politics that is more like people? The struggle of life is to realise and express the wonderful richness and fullness of our joint and shared humanity. Today we often confront a politics that constrains and restricts us, that is mechanical when it needs to be moral. There will be different and competing versions of the good society. We will have our tribes. But unless our tribe is open to challenge and change it will walk in tighter and tighter circles, and we will miss out on what it means to be fully human. And that would be a tragic waste of our lives and our times.

Neal Lawson

Introduction

The kind of conversation I'm interested in is one in which you start with a willingness to emerge a slightly different person ... it is always an experiment whose results are never guaranteed. It involves risk.

Theodore Zeldin, *Conversation*[1]

The origins of this book lie in a public debate I chaired for Compass in November 2013, between David Marquand and Hilary Wainwright. During the debate, we began to discuss what the good society meant to us, and the importance of pluralism, and a generosity and openness to new ideas and experiences, as opposed to tribalism.

A member of the audience challenged this, arguing that tribalism was too important to lose. 'It's what gets you out early in the morning in the snow to leaflet an entire ward.' Tribalism, he said, is about connectivity: a tribe is not just a restless group of global consumers, it carries a history and a sense of place, identity and traditions, a set of moral standards and rules that go beyond the law, a set of mutual obligations and a concept of responsibility and interdependence.

In the nineteenth century a 'tribal' solidarity enabled working-class communities to protect themselves; indeed my study of Southwark and Bermondsey in the 1920s described a tight-knit community pooling resources to improve health, housing and living standards.[2] Over time, however, that kind of solidarity has come to be seen as closed against strangers, narrow-minded, sexist and racist. As we sat in a draughty hall in one of the most diverse cities in the world it seems to have no place. But this has brought a new set of problems.

We talked in the meeting about whether, in the move towards open boundaries and open markets, we have lost too much of a sense of connectedness and belonging. As capitalism has globalised and markets have opened up, there has been a sense that perhaps too much openness without strong solidarities can make us feel lost and powerless. This sense of loss can lead us to turn in on ourselves, to become fearful of people different from us, to become narrow in our view of the world. We all want a sense of belonging that comes from kith and kin, a sense of home, and groups or clans that share our values and goals. And yet there is a parallel human yearning for adventure and change, for exploration and difference – the lure of new ideas and new experiences.

The impact of this tension can be felt in social policy, in the role of the state, in politics, in our personal lives, and in the world of work. What have we lost, and gained, as we trade solidarity for a sense of individual freedom? Could we, in this day and age, re-create a 'tribal' sense of togetherness without re-creating old insularities? Could we create an *open tribe*?

So began an enquiry – but I embarked upon it not simply through reading and research, but through a series of conversations with creative thinkers from all parts of the political spectrum – all of whom have engaged with this question. These were not conventional interviews, but open, fluid discussions with people who seemed to have things to say that were unusual and intriguing – they include politicians such as Jon Cruddas MP and Lisa Nandy MP, Baroness Lister and Lord Adebowale; academics such as David Marquand, Francesca Klug and Jeremy Gilbert; social entrepreneurs such as Hilary Cottam and Robin Murray; people who could talk from the perspective of Scotland, Wales and English local government, such as Willie Sullivan, Lee Waters and Councillors Janet Daby and Jack Hopkins; and young activists such as Carys Afoko and Rosie Rogers.

Why conversations? Well, because of a belief that the answers to these questions will come not from speeches, or monographs, but from a process of conversation, discussion and mutual learning – that if we are to learn to connect across different traditions and cultures we will do so through curiosity and listening. Conversation itself may prove to be part of the answer, and so the intention is to try out such an approach – in book form.

Each conversation has therefore been very open – allowing each participant to steer in whatever direction they choose. My role has been to ask the right questions and to probe for the stories, examples and practical ideas that could bring a 'new public philosophy', as David Marquand called it, alive.

I haven't offered each complete conversation, but used them as a starting off point for a different line of enquiry, drawing on the interviews to frame a set of questions connected to wider debates or beginning new lines of enquiry. Of course, it would be disingenuous to imagine that I have somehow been influenced by random ideas. I have chosen my interlocutors from among people I admire, people I think have interesting things to say, and whose ideas point in intriguing directions. I don't approach these issues without my own ideas, and I include in the conversations learning from my own research and experiences – including examples from practice both in the UK and abroad and quotations from recent authors such as Richard Sennett, David Goodhart and Manuel Castells, all of whom are writing about these themes.

During the conversations I learned a lot, changed what I thought and felt, and gained confidence about the need to change political behaviour 'from the bottom' – creating a new politics of social enquiry. As we become more and more disconnected from each other, and disconnected from our representatives at Whitehall, there is an urgent need to create democratic and social spaces where we can explore, learn about our differences, and begin to build solutions. So in Chapter Six I look at exciting examples of a different practice 'at the edge' and in Chapter Seven I explore how we could learn from this and begin to make change happen across the UK.

The following chapters draw together the conversations under a series of themes.

Chapter 1 – The Open Tribe

This chapter explores the twin ideas of 'tribe' and 'openness', looking at the impact of global economic change in opening up close-knit communities and breaking apart old solidarities, and at the rise of 'identity politics' from the 1970s onwards. I consider the argument of David Goodhart and others, that we tend to feel solidarity for 'people like us' and fear what we don't understand. In conversations with Lord Adebowale and Francesca Klug, I explore the re-emergence of a politics of fear and division. I also draw on a conversation with Robin Murray to explore the inherent human tensions between 'belonging and safety' and 'exploration and adventure'. We can become too safe, too closed, but societies can also be too open, without connectivity and belonging. We feel solidarities beyond our immediate friends and family around place and cause – and we may potentially belong to several 'open tribes', and form temporary connections which nevertheless build a wider sense of belonging.

Chapter 2 – What are we like?

This chapter examines assumptions about what humans are like – since this is a crucial question in rethinking politics. It draws from a conversation with David Marquand challenging the image of citizens as 'homo economicus' – interested only in the rational maximisation of economic self-interest. And it also draws on recent science that questions just how rational humans are; it explores the ways in which humans are 'more' than just rational, and seeks to capture the importance of imagination, empathy, judgement and creativity. Two questions emerge again and again in these conversations – 'what is it like to be fully human?' and 'how do we translate this idea into the world of public policy and politics?' I examine the possibility of using what Richard Sennett and others describe as 'dialogic' conversations to explore difference, to understand each other better without converging. This 'differentiated exchange' stimulates thinking about rather, than immediately solving, problems, creating puzzles, encouraging us to ask deeper questions – not simply of others, but of ourselves.

Chapter 3 – Why is politics so childish?

Chapter Three describes the infantilisation of national politics through the toxic domination of 'spin-doctors' and a hysterical 24-hour media, which reduces politicians' ideas to sound-bites and pre-scripted lines, making them, as MP Lisa Nandy says in my conversation with her, 'robotised'. Westminster politics tries to make political choices seem simple, rather than dealing with complexity. Through conversations with Lisa Nandy, Jon Cruddas, Natalie Bennett and Carys Afoko, I explore what politics would be like if it was opened up to a process of enquiry and examination, rather than trying to find simple solutions. The chapter looks at the experience of working across political parties, and the spaces opening up as politics increasingly engages people through action, campaigning and social movements rather than just voting. It examines the closed, inward-looking nature of political parties cut off from their supporters and the public. How would we make politics more grown up – more complex?

Chapter 4 – On the side of the people not the machine

Several of my conversations were about the world of work. And since work is often the most dominant aspect of our lives, it is important to think about how work impacts on our sense of belonging. Work is something fulfilling and creative at its best – and mind-numbing and degrading at its worst. What is it like to be fully human at work? The workplace democracy movement is all but dead, but lack of autonomy and creativity at work is now being identified as a cause of mental health problems as well as poor productivity. This chapter discusses the difference between good and bad work, and how we might make work a better part of our lives. Drawing on a conversation with Ruth Lister, I look at ways the balance between work and the rest of our lives might change. If we changed our work-life balance, might we change society? Can we begin to ascribe higher values to caring for the very young and the very old, and contributing to our communities? How do we create an open tribe where we value those whose work supplies us with the services and goods that we need – instead of treating them like servants? What would work be like if we brought our full human potential into the workplace? How might we change work to enable it to be a place of learning, exchange and creativity?

Chapter 5 – Can the state love?

In my conversations, a number of highly charged words came up over and over again – human, kindness, wisdom, grace, generosity – and love. In this chapter I explore some of the assumptions behind the current division between 'hard-working families' and 'benefit scroungers'. In a long conversation with Hilary Cottam, an anthropologist and social entrepreneur, we challenge the current preoccupation in the welfare state with 'keeping people out', and begin to explore an alternative which values personal qualities and strengths and tries to bring people in. To be fully human, we need to give and receive love. But as more and more of our lives are characterised by state intervention of one sort or another, and as a growing number of older, frail and ill people are dependent on the state for their care, it raises the question: can the state love? This chapter explores some of the values that underpin state intervention in our lives; the dangers of well-meaning performance regimes; and the difficulties of trying to 'treat everyone equally' – when we have different needs, backgrounds, hopes and dreams. If we are to learn to live as an open tribe, the state – local and national government – will have to play a part.

Chapter 6 – Change always starts at the edge

This chapter explores examples of where new ideas are already being put into practice. It considers innovation in Northern Ireland, Scotland and Wales and in English local government, as well as some interesting experiments in Europe – all of which access a more open and enquiring politics than the dominant style at Westminster. Innovative local politicians and managers are finding ways to listen to local people and co-create solutions that bring together public resource and community energy. I explore the beginnings of 'public-community' partnerships and the role of a 'fourth sector' – combining the best of entrepreneurial, public and community values. Finally this chapter looks at the prospects for 'social enquiry', building on Barry Quirk's idea of a 'civic square' to establish social and community spaces in which we could explore difference, and create a public dialogue about the sort of society we want to become – one that is tolerant and respectful of opposing views; while drawing also on the ideas of Jeremy Gilbert, and Chantal Mouffe's notion of 'agonistic democracy.'

Chapter 7 – 'We are the 99%'

In this chapter, I draw on an interview with Natalie Bennett, leader of the Green Party, who argues that 'the world we live in is neither natural nor inevitable'. In discussion with Lisa Nandy MP, Jon Cruddas MP, Carys Afoko and others I explore how change happens, and the scope to create what David Marquand calls 'a new social philosophy'. I draw on the recent work of Manuel Castells in documenting social movements that encompass both internet-networks and physical events such as consensus conferences, demonstrations and direct action. I also explore some of the building blocks for change – the way we make meaning, and interpret events; the scope to create a 'network of networks'; the role of social institutions in redefining and recreating themselves for the modern age; and the possibility of opening out both politics and government to a wider alliance of civil society organisations. Political party membership is shrinking as activism is growing. Can parties break out of their current, highly tribal, inward-looking preoccupations? Could they turn outwards and begin to connect to wider social movements? Local government and the voluntary and community sector regularly now use conversational techniques such as world café and open space. How could such spaces become part of what we understand as politics? Could we begin to treat social enquiry as an everyday way to solve problems? If we learned to listen to each other, and understood each other better, might we be on the way to creating an open tribe?

Conclusions

In the final chapter, I reflect on my own journey, and the experience of conducting an enquiry through conversation. Conversation changes politics, since ideas are built collaboratively. Good conversation doesn't necessarily mean that one side 'wins' or that agreement is reached, but it enables participants to better understand others, and themselves. I suggest that a different sort of politics would include a different media, challenging the sterile interviews we see on the television and radio, and the assumptions of print journalism. I explore the possibility of creating democratic and social spaces in which we can come together as citizens to explore difference – based on curiosity and a willingness to listen and explore. Finally I reflect on the ways that writing the book has changed me, as I think about my work-life balance and the courage needed to change things.

NOTES

1. Theodore Zeldin, *Conversation: How talk can change our lives*, Hidden Spring, Mahwah New Jersey 2000.
2. Sue Goss, *Local Labour and Local Government; A study of changing interests, politics and policy in Southwark 1919-1982*, Edinburgh University Press, Edinburgh 1988. For a much shorter version see Sue Goss; 'A New Jerusalem: Health Services in Bermondsey', in Simon Parker and Joe Manning (ed), *The History Boys; Lessons from Local Government's Past*, NLGN London 2013.

1. The open tribe

My conversation with Robin Murray, an industrial economist and intellectual innovator, helped me to think through what I meant by a tribe – and what I meant by an open tribe. He encouraged me to see that what was behind the concept was one of balance – between two compelling human imperatives: one towards connectedness and belonging, and the other towards exploration and adventure.

The term tribe has a long and chequered history as an anthropological, cultural and ideological term. Here I use it metaphorically to refer to a form of community that is based on belonging and a sense of kinship rather than the more impersonal forms of the modern state. In the West there is sometimes a distant sense of 'folk regret' for an earlier time when we imagine that people who lived together were connected by history, tradition and family, and collaborated together on a daily basis in the business of survival. But, as we shall explore, there were serious downsides to tight-knit communities. Our grandparents and great grandparents and great-great grandparents lived through a process that is still underway in some parts of the world, the growth of industrial society and a massive consequent population shift to cities. Here people can shake off their origins and choose different ways of making a living from those of their parents; but they also live in communities so large that they can't know everyone around them, where they live and travel constantly among strangers. In cities friends are chosen through shared interests, rather than necessarily being neighbours.

The sense of belonging and solidarity that we associate with the notion of tribe makes a lot of sense for subsistence farmers living in dangerous places: your kith and kin care for you, make sacrifices, help you in trouble and share your good fortune. There is perhaps also a stronger motivation to go beyond immediate self-interest and contribute to the greater good of the group. But boundaries are tight, and outsiders are clearly marked out. In city life, on the other hand, human solidarity stretches beyond kith and kin, and though it may be partial and patchy, it can move past a preoccupation with origin and birth, to a sense of place and loyalty – both to a community and to a shared set of beliefs and values.

A strong sense of exclusivity and belonging can be part of a shared religious, national or ethnic identity, and in the nineteenth century the rise of the nation state was reinforced in many European countries by a powerful national consciousness – a sense of national pride and often superiority. This national sense of 'superior identity' fed the colonial ambitions of western nations; it was this form of tribalism, transformed into nationalism, Richard Sennett believes, that led to the wars that destroyed Europe in the first half of the twentieth century: 'Tribalism couples solidarity with others like you to aggression against those who differ'.[1]

Human beings have always migrated, but contemporary global capitalism means that people now move across all the countries on the planet. Fervent nationalism still exists in the modern world, but in the aftermath of two world wars, the jingoistic self-congratulation of nineteenth- and early twentieth-century Europe elites has to some extent diminished:

> Complex societies like ours depend on workers flowing across borders; contain different ethnicities, races and religions; generate divergent ways of sexual and family life. To force all this complexity into a single cultural mould would be politically repressive and tell a lie about ourselves.[2]

WHAT DO WE MEAN BY 'OPEN?'

Robin Murray wanted to look at the beginnings of the contemporary use of the word 'open'. He traced it back to the development of the 'Open University' in the 1960s, when the idea of 'open' first began to mean moving beyond the boundaries of traditional institutions. He sees this as the start of the movement that saw younger people going up against established institutions of church, state, schools, the NHS ... And the word 'open' has gradually expanded in its use so that it can mean open source technology, open innovation, and now 'open health', which Robin says means 'thinking about health care that centres around individuals and families and not around conventional hospitals'. We discussed the fact that on a personal level 'openness' is almost always seen as good: 'open-hearted' and 'open-minded' are always seen as better ways of being than having closed hearts and minds. The word 'open' now carries with it a sense excitement about the future, a sense of forward movement. Open skies, open space, open landscapes – all symbolise our love of adventure. We see the limits of safety. We are curious. Openness can be about the space to explore – it carries meaning for many of us about escaping from 'closed' communities, small villages and parochial towns into the space and dynamism of great cities. Robin sees the pressure for openness as part of a wider transformation taking place in our society, reflected in the pressures towards open labour markets and open economies, and away from the constraints of more traditional societies.

But too much 'openness' also feels scary. Adventure on our own make us feel exposed, and we feel vulnerable if there is no-one looking out for us. For unprotected migrants, or for the very young or the very vulnerable, adventures in those open worlds can turn into nightmares. For those at the bottom of the heap, it is easy to be neglected or exploited in an open economy. Openness has also come to signify exposure, a lack of protection; a feeling that each individual has to fend for themselves in the system, as a small cog against the machine.

In an increasingly fragmented post-modern society, individuals float loose even of family, moving from city to city and country to country, replacing friends with Facebook contacts, romance with on-line dating, conversation with chat-lines in which no-one is exactly what they seem. Cash transactions begin to replace real bonds and reciprocity. It always seems to me tragic when the super-rich start listing their 'friends' as their personal trainer, their hairdresser and their make-up artist. In a post-modern dystopia we drift as lone individuals across the world-wide web – temporarily 'hooking up' with people, buying on the internet, chatting to strangers. Our interests become concentrated purely on ourselves – what can we buy, what can we eat, what should we wear?

SOLIDARITY AS PROTECTION?

The industrial revolution in the West opened up economies and society, creating great industrial cities to which agricultural workers were drawn in their millions – a casual labour market in which workers had no rights and little bargaining power, and where long working hours in vast dangerous factories became the lot of men, women and children. For the new working class, an intense solidarity was an essential way of building protection – and tribalism began to be used as a term to describe this strong shared interest of workers who might have come from Ireland, Scotland or any of the counties of England, but began to settle in new communities. People who a generation ago would have lived in villages and towns hundreds of miles away from each other began to form close-knit communities with a shared purpose, and combined to protect themselves and to develop a shared power that could match the power of capital – through trades unions, and working men's clubs, and through the co-operative movement. The new political parties, first the Liberal Party and then the Independent Labour Party and finally the Labour Party, became the political expression of this new sort of solidarity.

In my book *Local Labour and Local Government* I documented just such a solidaristic working-class community in Bermondsey.[3] The spread of trade unionism to the unskilled and semi-skilled workers of the docks and factories that lined the Thames gave a new confidence and sense of value to a very poor community. In this tiny docklands borough, the newly organised labour movement set up trades union branches, Trades and Labour Councils, a co-operative society, the Women's Co-operative Guild and the Federation of Women Workers. These organised the social life of the community, creating social clubs, football clubs, lectures, rallies, tea dances and socials. Few middle-class or even lower middle-class people lived here. Community politics reflected the tight-knit nature of the community; there were rigid social codes, an emphasis on self-help and self-reliance, and a sense of respectability and making a contribution, and of a self-organised community. This tribal politics was expressed by the Labour Party, which was connected into everyone's lives – by 1939 nearly one in ten of the population of Bermondsey was a party member. In my interviews with activists from the early twentieth century, they talked about a sense of everyone wanting the same things: 'We all grew up together, and the things we wanted were all the same; a decent place to live, an inside bathroom, central heating, security'.

By the 1980s this was beginning to fall apart, and the tribalism became self-defeating – a shrinking white working-class community 'contra mundum', unwilling to face change, feeling neglected and afraid of being overtaken by immigrant communities, trying to hold on to the past. David Goodhart, in *The British Dream*, argues that: 'One of the paradoxes of immigration is that the good strong communities that people on the left admire, with high levels of stability and mutual support, are, by definition, communities that are quite hard for outsiders to join'.[4] He argues that resistance to immigration has a legitimate community preservation aspect as well as the more obvious xenophobic dimension, and the two are often impossible to disentangle.

As new migrant communities arrived, they often had to rely on a sense of tribal loyalty and connectedness based on their country of origin – looking after each other, offering places to stay, helping fellow countrymen to find work and offering support in what could be a lonely and hostile environment. From both the older communities and the newer communities there was a longing for a sense of connectedness and solidarity: a sense of community belonging that is still strong for many of us. Jon Cruddas, in my conversation with him, talked about being feeling tribal:

> I'm quite tribal in my instincts. I live in gangs, tribes, teams and I quite like it, but I also like difference. I come from a big Irish Catholic family where there are strong ties of kinship and friendship, very tribal ... but in terms of aspirations, I'm struck by how similar the characteristics of the new migrants are to those of my

family ... we have the same patterns of kinship, the same sense
of what we want for our families, as the new arrivals coming to
east London now, the same ideas and same motivations ... but
not everyone can see the similarities.

THE GROWTH OF IDENTITY POLITICS

For some of my interviewees, the trades unions and labour movement were an important source of solidarity and belonging. But it
is easy to look back at working-class solidarity with a sense of
romance. It is easy to see our own communities as offering solidarity, help and a sense of belonging, while other people's
solidarities can seem defensive, even threatening. Victor Adebowale,
in my conversation with him, warns against too romantic an ideal
of the old labour movement. Working-class solidarity was often a
solidarity against new arrivals. The unions were uniting, and sometimes striking, against the employment of newly arrived immigrants
from the West Indies who were struggling to get jobs.

Francesca Klug, growing up in a North London Jewish community, felt we can also over-state that sense of 'closed' communities:
some communities were more fluid and open. In Hackney in the
1980s she remembers considerable harmony between communities, open and closed, mingling and mixing. She's not convinced
by the construct of harmonious insular communities:

> I'm not sure there isn't a mythical element to that sense of working-
> class solidarity – women may have been isolated while the men
> were down the pub ... actually communities were never just
> geographically based, there were always communities of class, of
> gender, of faith ... and the sense of being in a community is
> diluted through the sense of being in many over-lapping commu-
> nities – in my childhood, growing up in a north London Jewish
> community, it would have been very claustrophobic if I hadn't felt
> I had the power to choose to belong to other communities as well.

For the newer political movements in the 1960s and 1970s, solidarity was not simply about shared backgrounds or experiences,

but implied the process of constructing wider shared identities –
so that immigrants from many different places came to identify as
'black', while women from many different backgrounds began to
find a shared sisterhood. Victor Adebowale remembers the solidarity generated by early struggles against racism:

> The solidarity that makes sense to me is the 30 April anniversary
> of the Bristol bus boycott, the beginning of a race relations policy
> … the end of the notices in windows that said 'no dogs, no Irish,
> no blacks'. The black community created solidarity.

He also points to solidarity across communities: 'There have been
times, like Cable Street, when the east end community alongside
Jewish people fought the fascists'.

For 1970s feminists such as Purna Sen, Ruth Lister and myself,
an additional solidarity came from the women's movement. As
Purna says:

> The women's movement was the source of great support, a sense
> of finding yourself – wonderful. The sisterhood and solidarity
> that came from feminism was really important.

In the 1970s and 1980s these new solidarities began to fragment,
as arguments opened up differences in values or priorities.
Identities became more and more narrow, and we began to argue
about definitions, reducing our sense of affiliation to wider groups
– a process of fragmentation, leading to smaller and smaller groupings. As Ruth Lister comments:

> We came together as women and we thought that would be
> enough, and we thought that as women there would be solidarity.
> But over time it started to break down, because black women said
> you're not speaking for us; because most of us were white, and
> lesbian women thought that it was very heterosexual, and disabled
> women began to ask where the space was for them. It exploded in
> 1978 at national conference – in the end, this sort of identity poli-
> tics became a cul-de-sac.

In a massively diverse city like London, 'identity politics' carries dangers – confining us to smaller and smaller groupings of 'people like us'. As the group with whom we identify begins to narrow, instead of thinking in terms of 'women' or 'black people' we start to think about divisions of ethnicity, religion, sexuality and class, and each group begins to seek their own space, and holds conversations mainly with itself. This can translate into a dangerously fragmented political landscape – in which each 'community' looks after their own narrow interests, and national leaders, instead of offering ways to unite communities, find ways to divide them. Jon Cruddas warns about politicians treating each group of arrivals differently:

> Could you get the very worst kind of clan politics? Where you profile the communities and balkanise the landscape in order to harvest votes in fractured cities … creating the worst kind of pork-barrel politics, distributing resources to specific groups of voters demarcated on racial or religious grounds?

In the contemporary world, an appeal to 'tribe' is never anything other than constructed. Identity is no longer fixed or given, there are no natural solidarities: identity and solidarity are created through a process of shared understanding and collaboration. We have choices about whether we experience new arrivals or strangers as people 'like us' or as alien. That choice depends a lot on how we meet and experience others, and whether we meet them with open hearts, and open minds.

THE PROBLEM OF FEAR

Just at the moment, politics seems, in the UK, to be going through a particularly nasty stage. We are being invited to blame others for our problems. We are being told that, as 'hard-working citizens, we are being fleeced by free-loaders, by scroungers, by new arrivals. We are being encouraged to 'look after our own'.

As Gary Younge, writing in the *Guardian*, recently argued:

Our politics, particularly in an age of terror, austerity and growing inequality, is predicated on the basis that people are basically venial, selfish, dishonest and untrustworthy. The poor are assumed to be not looking for work but cheating on welfare, foreigners are assumed to be taking something from a culture rather than contributing something to it, public sector workers are assumed not to be devoted to public services but a drain on our taxes. The disabled are assumed to be well. When we look at others the default positioning of much of western political culture is not to see ourselves in them but to see a threat.[5]

He contrasts this with the action of Antoinette Tuff, the school book-keeper in the Discovery Learning Academy in Decatur, Georgia, taken hostage by a young mentally ill man with an AK 47 assault rifle, who talked him down, with love and compassion, and prevented anyone from getting killed.

David Goodhart worries that a growing tribal defensiveness will begin to break down the social contracts that implicitly underpin western welfare state societies. He suggests that people will care less about welfare if it's for people 'not like me'. For Goodhart the answer is to reduce immigration to a more 'manageable' level, and to strengthen our sense of shared citizenship. He argues for free English lessons, citizenship ceremonies, an end to segregated schools, and an end to what he calls 'single identity funding', where local authorities fund community centres and activities for individual ethnic communities. And while all these things may be worth doing in themselves, his focus is still on 'government action' rather than on challenging how we think or feel. It may be that we need to think more deeply.

Often the sense of solidarity and difference interact with each other in complex ways. Purna Sen talks about the fear of difference even within the international movement of women:

In the west you find the complete demonization of women who wear veils. In the Middle East or South Asia you find some very nasty comments about people who wear lipstick and nail varnish and high heels …

What causes division, she says, is the inability to step beyond your own experience:

> A lot of people who are very active on women's issues don't move beyond it to think about race or disability. In the same way, some people are active on LGBT issues but don't talk about class or race … true solidarity is an understanding of what other people's position feels like.

At the same time, Purna talks about the amazing courage shown by women in other parts of the world:

> There are women challenging violence when it is not safe to do so, being hugely courageous.

We discussed whether part of how we create openness is about challenging fear. Fear brings out the basest instincts, and narrows our sense of belonging to self-preservation. It follows that the open tribe will only stay open if we can create a society that protects us from the worst kinds of fear. To be safe from harm, from hunger, from attack – these things are important to enable us keep our optimistic spirit of discovery. But much of what we have to fear – to paraphrase – is fear itself. For people in western societies the fear they experience is disproportionate to any threat, and often displaced. Fear is about feeling out of control, exposed, unable to act, unable to defend. We are afraid of what we can't see, we are afraid of what we don't understand. But we know, because we had to experiment as children, that there are two responses to fear. One traps us, one liberates us. If we hear an unfamiliar noise in the middle of the night, the trapped response is to close up, to barricade ourselves into safe space, to huddle in bed, to lock the door and hope whatever it is goes away. That way fear grows. The liberating response is to investigate. To go, ideally with others, to see what that noise was, to find out that it was just a banging door – and then, instead of huddling all night in terror, we can relax, laugh, and go back to bed. If we investigate our fears, we can narrow them down, we can pinpoint real danger, we can become scientific in our responses. Fear is the nastiest of emotions. It limits us, it imprisons us. If we are fearful, we need, as a society to identify the sources of our fear, and to explore them. The less we know of other people's lives, the more assumptions we make, the less likely we are to be accurate. The alternative reaction to fear is curiosity.

We are, as a species, courageous. We don't like to be cooped up. Cowering in fear is never going to make us happy. The more we investigate, the more we meet other people, the more we discover that what holds us together is greater than what keeps us apart.

GETTING THE BALANCE RIGHT

In my conversation with Robin Murray I followed this exploration of the tension between 'openness' and 'tribalism' – which he sees as an example of a wider tension between order and chaos – between entropy, decay and dynamic force. An open economy is dynamic and creative, but also scary and exploitative; a closed system is controlling and deadening, but protected.

> In any system if you just have order, you have entropy – the death force – but if you only have dynamism, you have chaos without order … as the economy opens up, the subjectivity that comes from post-Fordism busting things open, that's scary – an open economy is scary – so how do you manage in an open system? You can't go back to a closed system, nor would we want to … but we have to respond in a new way … old closed institutions struggle as labour forces change and migration begins to interrupt old patterns.

We need to re-establish our solidarities, not in the old way, but through new connections between people. We can't simply fall back on tradition and history: these new belongings need to be created, positively, in ways that will work in the contemporary world. In my discussions, new solidarities seemed to emerge, not as powerful binary divisions, but as different ways of constituting a sense of belonging, ways that could reinforce, interrupt or challenge each other.

The first is a solidarity based on place – beginning with family, but stretching out to the community of people around us with whom we are interdependent, with whom we share schools and health facilities, parks and playgrounds, and to the parents of the children who go to school with our children, our neighbours, the frail old lady down the road, the people in the corner shop, the library. The solidarity of place will mean working alongside many people with whom we may not agree about much, and with whom we may not have much experience in common, but with whom we have social spaces in common, and the need to collaborate. For some in isolated rural communities this can mean working together to clear ice from shared roads, or helping to cut down trees that are blocking the way to the village; in cities this interdependence is less obvious and less keen, but it often means feeding each other's pets, collecting each other's children, and the shared duties of looking after neighbours, acting as school governors or organising a street petition.

Place remains very strong as a mobiliser in some communities. But as people commute longer and longer distances, and as they begin to live, work and have a social life in different districts or towns, the pull of 'locality' begins to lessen. These days we may find many different tugs on our attachment and our sense of belonging – we may have family in the US, and in Bangladesh, friends in Bradford and a community of work colleagues in London. We may have communities around our kids' schools, camaraderie around a political party and a football club, friendship systems in the village we came from, and a network of friends around our choir in Hackney. We tend to think of tribes as primarily geographical, but some people are becoming so mobile that for them there is no clear geographical sense of belonging. Increasingly, solidarity of place relies not on close-knit families and kinship, but on the active collaboration of people who may have come from very different origins – the weak social capital that enables our world to open out and touch other worlds. The more we draw on these connections, the easier it is to have both a sense of tribe and a sense of openness. If, as David Goodhart worries, we only talk to or look after or care about 'people like us', our ability to sustain community in the modern world diminishes.

As well as place, we draw on a second solidarity, that of cause: the values and beliefs that we share, the things we want to achieve, the changes we want to make. The causes that motivate us may be intimate and personal, or may be national or international in scope. Many of us devote many hours a week to the things we care about. We may belong to an environmental group tending woodlands or clearing ponds, we may coach football teams, keen to promote young talent; we may share a love of sweet peas or dahlias. Sometimes causes are altruistic or driven by personal tragedy, as with the Lawrence family, who dedicated decades to challenge police racism; or Kate and Gerry McCann's search for their child; the campaign groups that uncovered the neglect at Mid-Staffordshire hospital; all the expert patients and active pensioner groups. Sometimes the causes are intellectual or aesthetic – campaigning against ugly buildings or Tesco's stores; about embryology or GM crops; for or against women bishops.

Sometimes the cause is profound in its reach, and derives from faith or political ideology or passionately held belief. Activists in political parties have a fierce sense of cause that sustains them sufficiently to devote many years of their lives to knocking on doors and distributing leaflets. Solidarity based on cause can become an active process of connecting and constructing a sense of common good from passions and beliefs that might not, at first glance, have much in common. Instead of the breaking down and narrowing of identity that took place in the 1980s, we can envisage an opposite process of linking identities and finding the values that thread us together. Politics is always a process of building solidarities, not simply of responding to pre-existing solidarities, of creating connections between people who are quite different in the service of a shared endeavour that offers meaning and purpose.

The solidarity of values and cause can move us beyond the limits of shared experience to shared hopes and dreams. Ruth Lister and Purna Sen talked about the immense power and energy of the International Women's Movement; and Francesca Klug talked

about the connections and shared endeavour of the international
human rights movement ...

> which means we write letters on behalf of complete strangers to
> governments in distant countries, that we hold vigil for people
> we have never met. This is where solidarity draws on its broadest
> meaning ... when you step back from your narrow boundaries
> you realise how much you have in common.

These solidarities of place and value rub up against each other, and
can conflict. When we have created strong bonds of family and
place it can be difficult to rethink our boundaries, and to make
space for newcomers or for strangers.

Robin Murray tells the story of the old Italian industrial
districts, which became successful through a powerful set of inter-
connections and co-operative agreements. Farmers and small
businesses in tight communities, whose families had known each
other for generations, developed networks and cooperatives and a
complex set of interdependencies, helping each other out, sharing
loans, lending equipment, forming sales consortia – a very strong
sense of tribe:

> They would phone each other up and say 'I have an order that is
> too big for me, will you take half', knowing that the other will
> reciprocate in the future. But as borders opened, and with
> increased immigration, new arrivals from North Africa and East
> Asia reached as far into Italy as Emilia Romagna and Tuscany
> and began to set up their own small businesses. The old commu-
> nities were often proudly socialist with a strong belief in
> internationalism, but these were outsiders, so they struggled to
> know how to respond. How does the tribe respond to people
> who come from a very different culture? They didn't want to
> treat them as 'other', but didn't know these new people, and
> began to see them as a threat. So a man who ran one of the
> leading co-ops – a local co-operative bank – told me that they
> had a board meeting and discussed the issue for a whole day, and
> it was decided to go and talk to the new arrivals, and ask them

what their problems were. And it turned out that their major
problem was that when they sent money back home, up to fifty
per cent would get siphoned off by intermediaries. So the first
thing the bank did was to set up an arrangement whereby it took
only 5 per cent on such transfers, and that immediately began to
build trust ... and relationships followed ...

Robin says that it's a question of balance. Societies, institutions
and communities that are too closed cease to adapt and tend to
turn inwards and decay. But societies, institutions and communities that are too open can become inhuman, cruel, purposeless. We
need both a sense of tribe and belonging, and a sense of enquiry
and adventure. We can begin to see when we have gone too far in
either direction – and more importantly, we can begin to see what
is needed to regain balance. In each instance, in each society, we
can ask: 'do we need to increase our sense of belonging and connectivity – or do we need to challenge our assumptions and stretch
our minds?'

Shared values and beliefs help us find this balance. Robin
Murray talked about the abiding value of hospitality – not as an
act of generosity but as a dependable right. Hospitality enables
even closed societies to care for strangers, and makes it possible for
very poor people to travel when they need to, in the certainty that
they will be taken in and offered food. In poor societies we do
these things because we know that we may ourselves need that
help at some time in the future. Richard Sennett talks about reciprocal systems in China, when help is offered to someone and
repaid, not directly but to the next person within the network who
needs it – a long swooping reciprocity which works over time,
through trust and fellow belief.

At the same time we have values of curiosity and enquiry, a
fascination with strange lands and travellers' tales (though the
excitement of adventure in times gone by was too often furnished
to men by war); or there might be an attraction to the romance of
gypsy communities who refuse to be confined within a closed
village; and then there are the girls who run away to the bright
lights – or to the lure of the fairground. The anonymity of cities

has always offered a necessary refuge for the unconventional, for women who didn't want to marry, for single parents, gay men and women, transsexuals, for poets, adventurers and migrants, as well as entrepreneurs and chancers. The city supported the alternative values of independence, freedom, self-realisation. In cities we create new tribes – in friendship networks; clubs and societies based around a shared love of music, sport or dance; around lectures and learning, pubs and allotments; through politics, and through schools and community groups. And beyond all of these are the values that abide because of our shared humanity: the values that prompt us to rescue a fellow human being whom we have never met, to take in strangers, and to protect the weak and the old in all societies. As Robin Murray says:

> We think of the relationship between the individual and society as binary, but in fact it's not binary, it's a continuum, between the individual and various levels of tribe, moving from very close-knit communities to the Kantian notion of the universal connectivity of human beings. There are many intermediate forms of belonging and connectivity. Increasingly, we have tribes of value – not communities of interest. I don't like the word interest. Rather, it's about common values – and in the post-modern world we're in a number of tribes, and tribes we can move in and out of.

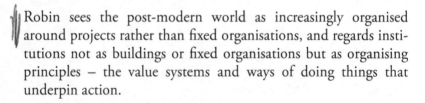

Robin sees the post-modern world as increasingly organised around projects rather than fixed organisations, and regards institutions not as buildings or fixed organisations but as organising principles – the value systems and ways of doing things that underpin action.

If you and I had a project to write a book, we'd come together and work very hard at it, and when it was finished we'd go our separate ways, but we'd remember it. It would be a temporary tribe, but we would know we could work together, and could do so again if the occasion arose. So the open tribe is a series of temporary but connected tribes that leave a memory.

If Robin is right, we can begin to see the emergence of open tribes rather than a single tribe, with weaker or stronger connections between them. The stronger our sense of who we are, and our own values, the more comfortable we can be in a vast, complex world. We don't have to choose between belonging and openness. The solidarities we need can be created in new ways.

NOTES

1. Richard Sennett, *Together: The Rituals, Pleasures and Politics of Co-operation*, Allen Lane, London 2012, p3.
2. Richard Sennett, *Together*, p4.
3. Sue Goss, *Local Labour and Local Government*, full reference in introduction.
4. David Goodhart, *The British Dream: Success and Failure of Post-war Immigrants*, Atlantic Books, London 2013.
5. Gary Younge, *Guardian*, 26.8.13.

2. What are we like?

Our view of 'what human beings are like' is profoundly important, because it limits and constrains what we believe people are capable of, and what matters to ourselves and others. David Marquand, in my interview with him, spoke about the terrible mistake we have made, across the capitalist west, in accepting 'rational economic man' (or woman) as a definition of what it is to be human. The idea of what David Marquand and others refer to as 'homo economicus' has come to dominate not just economic thinking but governmental thinking across all public policy. But, as David says, the danger with this is that we build:

> an incentive structure the presupposes that homo economicus is the only sort of person there is; and assume that we all respond to incentives and try to maximise our utility in the economic sense, and that that's what human beings are like – rational in the sense that economics defines rational … It builds in the assumption that there is only one way to organise things …

As he says, this is a dangerously flawed assumption. Humans are far more than simply rational computing machines, calculating the odds of every action as to whether it increases our wealth.

THE RISE OF 'HOMO ECONOMICUS'

Neoliberal economists assume that the citizen is a rational individual, making free judgements in an open marketplace to optimise their financial self interest. The world of work is treated as a process of exchange – we sell our labour power to buy commodities. The world outside this process of exchange is treated with suspicion, since in those areas of our lives that are not commoditised the true economic 'value' of things cannot be measured. Neoliberal economists are made anxious by the activities of families and social networks, or the public value created through collaborative action. In the early years of the Blair government, I remember the distrust with which Treasury officials responded to the idea of 'public value'. The freely offered help of neighbours or volunteers, the unpaid commitment of professionals and the relative cheapness of directly provided state services were all treated as 'distorting the market' – since they provided services 'below their true value'. So if the state, or a social enterprise, or you and I, can do something more cheaply than global corporations, we are seen, somehow, as cheating capitalism of its profits. David Marquand argues that the neoliberal governments of Thatcher and Reagan shifted the political language, and in doing so altered our sense of who we, the voters were, and what we wanted. This shift of language and identity is crucial, because it attempted to redefine the fundamental values that underpin governmental behaviour, and therefore politics.

If we believe that human beings are all simply 'rational utility maximisers', it becomes possible to argue that the vastly disproportionate rewards that come from capitalist accumulation are justified. Why should the state redistribute income, or enforce fairness? Those who are best at 'utility maximising' will survive at the expense of the others – why not cheat consumers, form cartels to fix prices, sell poisons dressed up to taste good, win millions on the stockmarket by destroying a country's economy, create toxic financial products and flog them before anyone notices? Who cares if other people suffer? If the price of staple foods rises in poorer countries, if fuel poverty increases, if people's savings are wiped out – they just didn't 'maximise their utility' well enough. Suckers!

But as David and I discussed, the values that underpin neoliberal economics are not values that most of us share. So why are they so dominant? Why do we allow them to determine economic and social policy? We know that we are not simply individuals acting alone. Nor are we making free decisions. We don't offer our labour into an equal and open market-place, and for many of the essential things we need to buy our choices are very limited. We know that in the private sector power is very unequal, and that individuals are constrained and controlled by the far more powerful companies. We know we are influenced by many things, not just economic rationality. Common sense experience tells us that most of us live our life with many goals, and few of them are primarily about wealth, or even about our work. And yet politicians address us as 'hard-working families' or as 'the squeezed middle' – not as caring children of frail parents, or as anxious mothers, or as potential tennis-players or bad poets. As David Marquand will argue in his forthcoming book:

> We need to challenge the economist's view of human beings, and how they behave. We need to rescue the extraordinary wonder of human beings from a view of them as simply 'rational utility maximisers'.

We are never, even in our highly commoditised world, motivated only by economic self-interest. As I write this I am listening to a radio report of the post office workers who turned down the offer of £2000 worth of shares on a point of principle.

'NOT EVEN THAT RATIONAL'

As psychologists and neurologists discover more and more about the human brain, we also begin to realise that human beings are not even very rational. Part of our brain is still the reptilian stem, capable of responding with ferocious energy to threat, fear and pain, but not very sophisticated. On top of that, we also have a powerful mammalian brain, capable of bonding, creating strong group loyalties and ties, passionately connected to our children and families, and capable of love, warmth, well-being. The frontal cortex, the youngest and least mature parts of our brain, hold our capacity for reason, calculation, assessment and judgement, but these are not always the parts of us that are dominant. Advertisers have known for decades that you can sell products that are bad for people by appealing over the frontal cortex straight into the pleasure-gratification parts of the mammalian brain!

Even more interestingly, psychologists are learning that even the parts of the brain responsible for reasoning don't always reason very well. In their book *Nudge*, Thaler and Sunstein showed the short-cuts we make, and the often unfounded assumptions we make.[1] We are lazy, we take short-cuts, we are often content to do things just because others are doing them; we rely on a default set of judgements and values, and don't change them very often.

Nudge introduces two sets of protagonists, 'econs' and humans. Econs respond in the fully 'rational' self-interested way that economists would predict. But humans don't. Thaler and Sunstein suggest that to help people to be fully rational, governments should support them with 'choice architecture' – a benign process of helping people to make good choices.

Daniel Kahneman's research shows that while we have a thinking system capable of calculation and careful analysis, we don't use it much. We rely far more on our 'system 1' thinking – our intuition, which is fast, originates impressions constantly, is freewheeling and impulsive, our 'gut feeling'. This is based on a build-up of experience and a set of assumptions, rather than an accurate analysis of any single situation. As Kahneman says, 'humans are not well described by the rational-agent model'.[2] We don't read the small print on contracts; we hope for the best in our financial affairs; we don't protect ourselves from fraud and charlatans. This is important, because as Kahneman says:

> The assumption that agents are rational provides the intellectual foundation for the libertarian approach to public policy; do not intervene with the individual's right to choose unless the choices harm others. Libertarian policies are further bolstered by admiration for the efficiency of markets in allocating goods to the people who are willing to pay the most for them.

Kahneman's conclusions are low-key and benign in a similar way to those of the *Nudge* authors. He recognises that humans need protection from others who deliberately exploit their weaknesses, and especially the quirks of 'system 1' and the laziness of 'system 2'. He also expresses some hope that 'organisations are better than individuals when it comes to avoiding error, because they naturally think more slowly and have the power to impose orderly procedures'; and he suggests that organisations could encourage a culture in which people watch out for one another as they approach minefields.

But Margaret Heffernan, in her book *Wilful Blindness*, shows that organisations are often worse than individuals in identifying mistakes. She traces the power that organisational cultures have to create 'group think', either because challenge or doubt is punished by managers, or because teams and groups reinforce assumptions and norms, or because professionals close ranks to protect each other. Psychologists have shown through a series of studies that in situations where an individual, acting alone, would recognise something as wrong, in organisations we often ignore such evidence. She gives a series of chilling examples of situations when people in organisations fail to tell their bosses when things are going wrong:

> Ideology and orthodoxies powerfully mask what, to the un-captivated mind is obvious, dangerous and absurd ... fear of conflict, fear of change keeps us that way; almost all employees believe their bosses do not want to hear the truth. An unconscious (and much denied) impulse to obey and conform shields us from confrontation and crowds provide friendly alibis for our inertia. And money has the power to blind us, even to our better selves.[3]

The implosion of the mortgage industry in the US was a good example. Financial institutions displayed at all levels a staggering degree of 'wilful blindness', and while many individuals now say they knew things were wrong, the norms and assumptions and shared greed made it impossible to challenge.
Competition didn't help:

> Competition between the participants was so fierce that instead they all copied each other. The drive to compete just created more and more uniformity. It wasn't just that everyone was working from the same assumptions; they all used the same software ... (p189)

... In their mutually reinforcing conformity, each of these businesses perpetuated and exacerbated each other's errors and flaws until they comprised a system that could not change without collapse (p191).

So, even if the world was a safe place for individuals to make rational decisions about economic optimisation, we wouldn't do it very well.

And we also know that, in reality, the world we live in is dangerously unequal, with power concentrated in a very few hands. Individually we have very little power to change the terms of the choices we are offered.

THE ONGOING BATTLE FOR THE HUMAN

There is a much greater challenge to the model of 'homo economicus' than the fact that we turn out to be not very rational. More important, much more important, is the realisation, spoken of by almost all my interviewees, that a purposeful and valued life is not primarily about economic self-interest. It's not just that humans are less than rational; we are also, crucially, more. Victor Adebowale talked about 'the ongoing battle for the human'. So what do we mean by this? What is at stake in this 'ongoing battle for the human'?

The uniquely human part of our brain gives us more than the power to solve puzzles, to make judgements, to calculate. It gives us imagination. We can imagine a time other than our own; we can invent futures; we can live through the experience of others. We have always told and understood stories about different lives than our own. Through story we can empathise with others. Our great human gifts include our ability to sing, climb mountains, dance, cook, garden, invent and play games, competitive and uncompetitive, write poetry, solve puzzles, tell jokes. Life is made worthwhile by warmth, good food, fellowship, freedom, a sense of personal worth and purpose. To limit our humanity to the very narrow group of decisions that affect our economic well-being is to crush us back into being little more than beetles, scurrying around, simply surviving. It is many decades since Maslow developed his hierarchy of needs – and yet in 2013 we hear the sorry tale of government ministers justifying spending on the arts simply through the economic growth it generates.

Anyone with any experience of creativity knows the deep joy that comes from using our imaginations to make music, drama, art, or a garden. Anyone with craft skill knows the intense pleasure that comes from making something with our hands. The human rights movements stems not from self interest but from the sense of importance of every single human being.

Francesca Klug in her interview talked about the need to wonder at another person:

> We need to pay attention to the magic that is a human being – what it is that makes us human – that's what attracted me to human rights, an ethical, spiritual conception of the human spirit. I've felt disappointed with the left, given all the talk about 'the people', for not being more people-centred … the core history of human rights is not simply about legality, but is about philosophers listening to the voices of people, and trying to identify what it meant to be human.

The complexities and ambiguities of our lives, loyalties, loves – are better represented in literature, in poetry and in song than they are in government policy documents or political tracts. Myth, story and poetry are able to deal with contradictions and paradox; they let us look at problems and dilemmas without trying to solve them. The ability of a story to show us the tensions and dilemmas in our lives, to help us sit with them, to enable us to just 'be', is often more powerful than trite advice or simplistic solutions. Humans may not always be rational, but we are capable of being meta-rational – able to transcend linear ways of thinking and to connect directly through our hearts and our spirit with other ways of seeing, and to deeper sources of meaning. We can still watch a Greek tragedy and be moved by it, even though the writers lived thousands of years ago in a society we can barely imagine. Shakespeare can still speak to the dilemmas and choices that we face in our modern lives, while scientific text books from a few decades ago have only historical relevance.

For people of faith, there is an additional depth, that of religious belief. Religious belief is often immensely comforting, but it can also be challenging: some religious people have a moral courage that makes them stand out. There are as many different sorts of religious people as there are different atheists. Religion can be deeply conservative, increasing divisions and separating people along 'tribal' lines, but it can also be open, a source of enquiry and exploration. Some religious leaders reach out for dialogue when less courageous people are becoming defensive and closing in. When Pope Benedict XV1 offended Muslims in a speech at Regensberg, by quoting a medieval text which attacked Muslim jihadism and violence, the response of Muslim Tariq Ramadan was to go and meet the Pope to begin an open enquiry:

> The overall consequences [of the Pope's words] prove more posi-
> tive than negative ... our constructive dialogue on shared values
> and ultimate goals is far more vital and imperative than our
> rivalries and sterile competition over exclusive possession of the
> truth ... It is essential that each of us sit down at the table with
> the humility that consists in not assuming that we alone possess
> the truth, with the respect that requires that we listen to our
> neighbours and recognise their differences, and finally, the coher-
> ence that summons each of us to maintain a critical outlook in
> accepting the contradictions that may exist between the message
> and practice of believers ...[4]

We easily create religious stereotypes and make assumptions about the social attitudes linked to belief, but, as with our other assump-tions, we are often wrong. The Catholic church spans a range of views from social and political conservatism to support for revolu-tionary movements in Latin America. The Church of England includes both strongly social conservative and strongly libertarian views. There is a movement in both older Muslim societies and newer Muslim communities towards an egalitarian Islam, and Islamic feminism is growing, calling for a secular state and an end to dichotomies between east and west. Increasingly people are moving between countries and continents and are shaped by, and identify with, diverse cultures. Many people have to negotiate the multiple identities we possess, and find ways to be true to their religion, their social values, their families and friends, and to themselves.

Religious networks, virtual and real, are creating space for face to face debate and collaboration to find new interpretations – moving beyond custom and practice from the distant past, and from some of the assumptions built into multicultural policies of the twentieth century.

For many of us who don't believe in a god or take part in a single religion, there is often, all the same, a strong spiritual sense that humanity is connected through the generations to our very beginnings and into the future – and that such a connectedness is sacred. There is a sense in most of us, perhaps, that we owe it to our humanity not to simply live a base life, but to love, to care for others, to create beauty when we can, to revel in the beauty of our planet and to protect it. Rowan Williams, speaking in 2013 at the Edinburgh International Book Festival, argued that spiritual care meant tending to every possible dimension of a sense of the self and each other – it was about 'filling out as fully as possible human experience'.

A sense of wonder at other human beings does not require religious faith. As imaginative creatures, we are able to understand how it might be to be someone else, to see into the future, to gain an insight into the lives of people who lived thousands of years ago. Through fiction, we can explore imaginary worlds, and understand things that we have never experienced. We have the power of invention. And while all creatures may, in some way, celebrate being alive, humans have the capability to celebrate the 'aliveness' of our existence in poetry and music, in theatre and art, in ways that no other creature on this planet can do. Each human being has seen things or thought things in ways that are not entirely the same as the thoughts or ideas of anyone else.

I remember reading, as a teenager, the famous George Orwell essay 'The Hanging', and was reminded of it when trying to write this chapter, both because of what it says about human beings, and because it shows us the ability of literature to change the way we think and feel – in a way that legislation and policy papers cannot. The essay was published in 1931, after Orwell had served in the imperial police force in Burma. This extract comes as he escorts a prisoner to the gallows:

> It was about forty yards to the gallows. I watched the bare brown back of the prisoner marching in front of me. He walked clumsily with his bound arms, but quite steadily, with that bobbing gait of the Indian who never straightens his knees. At each step his muscles slid neatly into place, the lock of hair on his scalp danced up and down, his feet printed themselves on the wet gravel. And once, in spite of the men who gripped him by each shoulder, he stepped slightly aside to avoid a puddle on the path.
>
> It is curious, but till that moment I had never realized what it means to destroy a healthy, conscious man. When I saw the prisoner step aside to avoid the puddle, I saw the mystery, the unspeakable wrongness, of cutting a life short when it is in full tide. This man was not dying, he was alive just as we were alive. All the organs of his body were working – bowels digesting food, skin renewing itself, nails growing, tissues forming – all toiling away in solemn foolery. His nails would still be growing when he stood on the drop, when he was falling through the air with a tenth of a second to live. His eyes saw the yellow gravel and the grey walls, and his brain still remembered, foresaw, reasoned – reasoned even about puddles. He and we were a party of men walking together, seeing, hearing, feeling, understanding the same world; and in two minutes, with a sudden snap, one of us would be gone – one mind less, one world less.[5]

It is the recognition that in every human being there is a whole world that has stayed with me. Treating others as an end in themselves, rather than a means to an end.

When I asked David Marquand how he defined the good life, he answered:

> a society in which people are treated as an end in themselves rather than as a means to an end.

That belief, simply stated, offers a powerful test – of work, of government action, of individual and group behaviour. We should each, argued many of my interviewees in their own way, be able to become the person we are capable of being. We should not be constrained, controlled or used simply for the pleasure or gain of others. These values are different from the careless certainties of the twentieth-century right- and left-wing movements. People are not to be treated as pawns in a greater game, so that their experience and beliefs can be dismissed as 'collateral damage' or 'false consciousness'. Human rights values emerged in the aftermath of the holocaust and world war two, but, as Francesca Klug says, we have yet to live the values of human rights in all aspects of western democracies. Our laws protect human life and freedom, but we have accepted a very limited version of both.

If we were to have a deeper, richer view of what it is to be human, what would be the consequences? We would probably ascribe greater value to the security, well-being and comfort we gain through our relationships with friends and family. But the 'ongoing battle for the human' involves far more than simply being comfortable with what we already have. It means moving past simplistic formulations of our base interests as being simply about survival, money and possessions, and stretching ourselves to find out what we are capable of becoming.

Most of us know the joy that comes from being truly heard. Understood. But even in families it doesn't happen very often. In communities, in our wider social and political organisations, it happens hardly at all. It is the complaint most often made of the political process – that no-one is listening. But if we want to be heard, we need to recognise that desire in others. We each feel that we are more complex, sophisticated and unique than is reflected in the way we are treated by the state, by corporate organisations, by strangers. We know that our experience and our wisdom make our stories worth listening to. But we tend to take short-cuts with other people, quick to rely on stereotypes, to make assumptions. If we were truly to live these values we would be more curious about the worlds that exist inside the imagination and experience of others. We would see imagination not simply as the privileged possession of artistic or creative types, but as an important part of everyone's being. We would value it. We would make space for it. We would try to make room for everyone to practise their imagination and creativity. We would feel a collective sense of guilt that for many people in a modern rich western democracy, working hours blot out almost everything but labour.

Curiosity about the 'worlds' that are other people leads to a different sort of encounter: as well as the familiar and reinforcing conversations between close friends and family, there can be a generous enquiry between strangers. Instead of accepting a world in which we live alongside people with very different lives without connecting, we would try to find out more about each other. We would strike up conversations. We would make fewer assumptions and ask more questions. We would read more books written by people with different lives, or watch their films or plays. We would open ourselves up to the different worlds around us. We might not all be able to afford to travel, but there are a hundred different worlds in our own neighbourhoods. In those encounters we would find people who need our help – and we would also find people who could help us. We would develop a stronger sense of reciprocity, of mutual understanding, of respect.

Some of my interviewees talked about finding the similarity between people and of course finding our common humanity is important. But since humans like excitement and adventure, we need not be so quick to assume everyone is the same.

In his book *Together* Richard Sennett talks about difference as a source of fascination and interest. It can be intriguing and enjoyable. He says it would be a mistake to pretend there are no differences, but in any case that would be a sad thing, because those differences are fascinating. For Sennett conversation is a crucial form for exploring difference He talks about two different sorts of conversations, the dialectic and the dialogic:

> In dialectic ... the verbal play of opposites should gradually build up to a synthesis; dialectic starts in Aristotle's observation in the Politics that 'though we may use the same words, we cannot say we are speaking of the same things – the aim is to

come eventually to a common understanding.' Skill in practising dialectic lies in detecting what might establish that common ground ... Another type of skill appears in the Platonic dialogues, where Socrates proves a very good listener by re-stating 'in other words' what his discussants declare – but the re-statement is not exactly what they have actually said, or indeed intended. The echo is actually a displacement. This is why dialectic in Plato's dialogues does not resemble an argument, a verbal duel ... rather misunderstandings and cross purposes come into play, doubt is put on the table; people have to listen harder to one another.[6]

So this kind of dialectic conversation is precious, moving us past simply shouting, or getting stuck by restating our position, enabling us to listen carefully enough to reframe, move sideways, come at things in different ways in order to detect the common ground behind the actual words. A dialectic conversation is one in which each person moves towards each other, learns, changes, and finally reaches a shared understanding.

But Sennett is more interested in 'dialogic conversations' – conversations that don't resolve themselves in that way:

Dialogic is a word coined by Russian literary critic Mikhail Bakhtin to name a discussion that does not resolve itself by finding common ground. Though no shared agreements may be reached, through the process of exchange, people become more aware of their own views and expand their understanding of one another.

In a dialogic conversation, people may spark off each other, or go off at a tangent, or tell stories. And tellingly, says Sennett, 'a dialogic conversation can be ruined by too much identification with the other person' (p21). In this context empathy is more important than sympathy. Both imply recognition, but 'one is an embrace and the other an encounter' (p21). Sympathy overcomes differences through imaginative acts of identification; empathy attends to another person on his or her own terms. Sympathy has usually been thought a stronger sentiment than empathy, but, says

Sennett, 'I feel your pain' puts stress on what I feel, it activates one's own ego. 'Empathy is a more demanding exercise, at least in listening; the listener has to get outside him- or herself' (p21). Empathy enables us to connect to others without imagining ourselves to be like them. It's a less close connection; it opens us up to greater discomfort and to challenge – since we might find ourselves learning about experiences that seem alien, or ways of thinking that we don't share – but it enables us to respect and value others even when their lives are very different. It doesn't always lead to shared view or agreed action, but it does lead us to understand ourselves and others better.

Sennett distinguishes between altruism – which requires win-win – and differentiated exchange, where strangers meet, talk and come away with a sharper understanding of themselves. These broader encounters between worlds stimulate thinking rather than solve problems; they create puzzles, they encourage us to ask deeper questions, not simply of others, but of ourselves.

Which brings us back to diversity. Theodore Zeldin argues that the best conversations are with people who are different:

> Conversation is a meeting of minds with different memories and habits. When minds meet, they don't just exchange facts; they transform them, reshape them, draw different implications from them, engage in new trains of thought. Conversation doesn't just reshuffle the cards: it creates new cards ... It's like a spark that two minds create.[7]

Zeldin argues that the most valuable conversations are 'meetings on the borderline of what I understand and what I don't, with people who are different from me'. Margaret Heffernan sees this conversation from difference as a way of helping to keep us safe. Diversity, she argues, is our best protection against 'wilful blindness'. If we want to build greater awareness of the world around us:

> We can start by recognising the homogeneity of our lives, our institutions, neighbourhoods and friends, putting more effort into reaching out to those who don't fit in and seeing positive

value in those that prove more demanding. Looking at any of our major institutions, from parliament to corporate boards, think tanks and churches – that homogeneity suddenly looks like a weakness and a risk. Diversity, in this context, isn't a form of political correctness but an insurance against the internally generated blindness that leaves these institutions exposed and out of touch. The very fact that these groups feel comfortable should ring alarm bells (*Wilful Blindness*, p300).

We make ourselves powerless when we choose not to know. But we give ourselves hope when we insist on looking – when we begin the process of enquiry. Wisdom, Heffernan argues, 'starts with the question: "what could I know, what should I know, that I don't know?"'.

The way we relate to each other either strengthens divisions or creates bridges so that we can begin to explore. We need both dialectic and dialogic conversations, both sympathy and empathy. But the values that David Marquand and Francesca Klug espouse – treating every human being as of immense value in and of themselves rather than as a means to an end – underpin both.

Living by these values doesn't, of course, do anything to make easier the challenges our civilisation faces. Resources are scarce, people's needs collide, our beliefs conflict. Nothing here changes the difficult choices we face. But it might change the way choices are made.

NOTES

1. Richard Thaler and Cass R. Sunstein, *Nudge: Improving Decisions about Health, Wealth and Happiness*, Yale University Press, New Haven and London 2008.
2. Daniel Kahneman, *Thinking Fast and Slow*, Allen Lane, London 2011, p411.
3. Margaret Heffernan, *Wilful Blindness*, Simon and Schuster, London 2012, p4.
4. *Guardian*, 3.11.13.
5. George Orwell, 'The Hanging', first published in 1931 in *The Adelphi*.
6. Richard Sennett, *Together*, pp18-19.
7. Theodore Zeldin, *Conversation*, Hidden Spring 2000.

3. Why is politics so childish?

In every other sphere of human activity, we recognise, as adults, the complexity of the world we live in, the hard work that is needed to forge successful relationships, the nuances of careful diplomacy and the multi-faceted nature of every problem – but not in politics. The toxic interface between Westminster spin-doctors and a hysterical twenty-four hour news machine has infantilised politics to the point where we are treated to nodding dog politicians unable to express themselves beyond the repetition of a script written by inexperienced advisors; where the difficult dilemmas of our time are reduced to sound-bites, and solutions are produced in the form of slogans – 'the something for nothing society', 'the squeezed middle', 'hard-working families'.

So I thought I would talk to some of the more creative politicians in the UK, in an attempt to explore politics from the standpoint of the open tribe. I spoke to Jon Cruddas, Lisa Nandy, Natalie Bennett from the Green Party, Victor Adebowale and Ruth Lister from the House of Lords.

Jon Cruddas had a memorable phrase about 'stopping the transmission of the fixed answer'. It made me ask, 'what are the right questions?' How do we find questions wide enough and profound enough to guide us through the coming century? When I asked Jon what he thought the right question was, his reply was surprising. He said: 'How do you allow people to live more virtuous and self-fulfilled lives?' That is a great question. And it's not the sort of questions politicians usually ask.

Victor Abedowale, a cross-bencher in the House of Lords, talked about the need to 'stop trying to simplify things. Politicians in the old mould continue to tell people they can have a world that is simple'. Our conversation took place on a day that UKIP was in the news following election wins, and Victor commented:

> That's what UKIP are doing, continuing to make things simple for people – saying 'the problem is immigration' or 'the problem is Europe'. But life isn't simple. We need a politics that brings people to complexity.

Lisa Nandy talked in my interview with her about the frustration of over-control:

> One of the problems for all the major political parties is the centralisation of politics, which coincided with media control and the need to have a clean, coordinated message. We've ended up in a position where we're all supposed to pretend that we agree with each other all the time ... which is absurd. Some of the decisions are hugely complicated and there are many sides to an issue ... I think people would be hugely reassured to know that real debates are being had, not just between political parties, but within them ... that we understand the complexity of what we're dealing with.

So how did we get to here?

Of all the spheres of life, politics is perhaps the most tribal. After all, political parties need to defeat each other at elections, and this makes us assume that a vicious adversarial exchange is inevitable. The metaphors for politics are often violent – attack, damage, strike, tanks, armies – politics is war through peaceful means. Media stories are always biased towards conflict, the exposé, back-biting, scandal. 'Sensible people exchange views and build a consensus' is never going to be news.

And the antagonism between political parties is, of course, often profound. It is not too much to say that followers of one political party may hate followers of another. People passionate about their beliefs are angry about, and often dismissive of, counter-beliefs. Political parties often 'stand for' powerful and conflicting interests. In the early years of the twentieth century, British society saw

itself as divided into two great classes, each represented by a political party. In the 1950s and 1960s, parties talked about weighing
votes in certain constituencies rather than counting them. In the
interviews I conducted in Southwark in the 1980s, party old-
timers said, 'people round here knew that the Labour Party was for
them and the Tories were against them'. I noted down that one
party activist said – with pride – 'In those days you could put a red
ribbon round a poodle and they'd elect him'. This tribal certainty
had real advantages, because the parties didn't need to communicate the subtlety of differing policies – the party story could be
broad brush: Labour 'stood for' the working man, while the Tories
'stood for' the middle classes. Assumptions about what each party
would do in office could be derived from underlying values and
principles: Labour would nationalise, extend workers' rights, tax,
and build a welfare state; the Tories would do the opposite.

As the ties between class and voting (which of course had
never been completely watertight) loosened, the tribal instincts
of the electorate began to shift. By the 1970s, it was harder to see
the line between middle-class and working-class aspirations, and
in marginal constituencies the two main parties began to worry
about the elusive 'Mondeo man'. Growing affluence started to
make old certainties less certain. Skilled working-class people
earning a decent wage began to feel that they had less in common
families on benefits, and more in common with those who
wanted to own their own home. Many long-term Labour
supporters resented the sheer inefficiency and bad temper of
some parts of the public sector, which seemed to eat up so much
of their hard-earned wages, and only the Tories were willing to
talk about this. At the same time, many middle-class people –
women, gays and lesbians, those from ethnic minorities – found
no home in the close-minded and backward looking Tory Party
of Tebbit and Thatcher. The problems of society began to seem
more complex than the 'two legs bad four legs good' formulae of
tribal politics. Ironically, as the electorate began to become more
open and more questioning, the parties themselves became more
inward-looking and more factional. Labour tore itself apart
during the Thatcher years, while the Tories became ever more

regressive and blinkered – parties talked more and more to themselves and less to the electorate, defending a tribal loyalty that was coming unstitched.

POLITICS A 'PRODUCT'

By the 1980s and 1990s, political parties were changing. The Conservatives had never invested in party democracy, and under Blair the Labour Party abandoned the idea of a democratic party conducting a dialogue with its membership. Both main parties turned to marketing experts and began to treat voters as consumers of corporate products. With a strong company party 'brand' created by clever marketing, their aim was to respond to consumer 'demand' understood through polling, focus groups and market testing. Communication was controlled by spin-doctors, who market-tested language and phrases, and integrated Westminster politics with the, by now, 24-hour media: they planned their 'image making' with military precision, through interviews, photo-opportunities and sound-bites. Instead of policy developed by expert civil servants in government and through resolutionsto party conference in opposition, policies became 'products' – designed by spin-doctors, market-tested with focus groups, and sold with a carefully scripted marketing patter which all politicians had to repeat. Market tricks such as pledge cards were adopted to strengthen the 'customer base'. Westminster became a supermarket in which competing political brands tried to attract votes through clever packaging of almost identical political wares. The policies of each party were no longer honed through debate and discussion, or derived from the values and logic of a wider set of social institutions and social movements in which the party was based. It became impossible to guess what policies each party would pursue, so indistinguishable had the rhetoric become. Policies were kept under wraps and launched with all the flummery of Steve Jobs launching a new Apple product – with a great 'reveal' at party conference.

As a way of doing politics this is bizarre. Ideas are not products to be consumed; they are always necessarily about learning, exchanging, exploring, digesting; as individuals we need to process an idea carefully before we accept it. The more we think about it, the more we talk about it, the more carefully we will consider its merits and grow to understand it. An idea launched 'cold' seems to us un-thought out, because we haven't thought it – not yet. Over time we get used to it: ideas take time to take hold.

Marketing aims straight for our childlike mammalian brain – promising comfort, instant gratification, reassurance, familiarity. It's great at selling chocolate, drink, holidays or cosmetics. But if we want people to explore new and difficult problems we need them to engage with their imagination, their analytical brain, their capacity to explore and judge – the frontal cortex. It is the powerful cognitive element of political work that is being abandoned. And we humans often resist hard work. We like comfort. New ideas don't come easily. New solutions evolve at the edge of what we are capable of, and can be discomforting. But that doesn't mean that we humans are not capable of creative, difficult thought, nor that we can't recognise the need for it. Treating ideas like chocolates is treating us like children.

MAKING POLITICS WORK BETTER

The politicians with whom I spoke had been thinking hard about what would change things. The first, and perhaps most obvious, suggestion is to bring back party democracy. The Liberal Democrats still have a democratic process of policy formation, and while that doesn't make their lives comfortable, it means there is still a connection between members and the leadership. In both the Labour and Conservative Parties there is now no sense of being able to influence the party leadership. Treating policies as 'product launches' at national conferences – keeping them secret until the last minute – has been catastrophic for party members, who not only feel they have no influence on their own party views, but are also helplessly unable to explain their party policies on the doorstep. How on earth can the hapless foot-soldiers persuade people to vote for their party when they have only the haziest of ideas about what their party stands for? Is Labour planning to be tough on welfare claimants at the next election, or to be compassionate? Will the Tories cherish the NHS or privatise it? Take us out of Europe, or campaign to stay in? Will the Liberal Democrats abolish tuition fees or raise them? No wonder membership of the mainstream parties has crashed.

Lisa Nandy talks about Labour Party members and local people feeling shut out of decision-making and influence, excluded by the banality of the debate where only one corner of public affairs is up for discussion, among parties that agree on all but the detail, while a vast swathe of public policy has become undiscussed and undiscussable.

But the malaise goes deeper than that. While some local parties are energetic and creative, many are still tribal, defensive and inward-looking. I decided to talk about this with Carys Afoko, who has just started working for a MP in Westminster:

> The barriers to entering politics are pretty high if you don't already know people. When I volunteered on a campaign in America everyone that walked into the field office was given a warm welcome, everyone was 'hi, glad you could make it, great that you've joined us'. But in the UK, often you shuffle into a meeting and no-one tries to make you feel welcome or as if you should be there ... So then the only people coming into politics are people like me who had parents who introduced them to politics, or people brave enough to push past the pain barrier. That's why you get the same sort of people all the time ... people who are confident or have a sense of entitlement – and they are often relatively privileged. People who didn't grow up with politics, people who lack confidence, find that there's no-one like them, or who looks like them, or if they pluck up the courage to get involved they find they're not welcome.

It is not just the political parties that feel alien and unwelcoming – the same can be true of trades unions, and social institutions. Rosie Rogers, grass roots activist and co-ordinator of Compass, talks about her experience as a young activist of joining a trades union:

I didn't join a trade union for what I'd get out of it in return. I wanted to show solidarity with the people who need it. And I felt that this was a diverse place because it is connected to working people and people from different backgrounds, and the people who really need help when they get sacked or mistreated. The union seems to be rooted in the same values as mine, but it's not a fun place, it's not welcoming or creative or open to anything new. These older networks – the reason I don't get involved is because of the hierarchies and the structures. It's always loud, confident men calling the shots, not just at the top but at branch meetings. Labour organisations seem to have so much baggage, they are so tribal, and, while I agree with the values and believe in what they say they believe, they don't act on it, and they don't communicate it … they don't excite me …

She says that she always feels that she is 'in the shadow of the baggage of years of defeat':

The labour movement seems so full of pain and hurt – always saying 'we tried that before' or 'we could never do that' – it's as if they don't have any trust in anything new. Older people, people of my mother's generation and before, had some of the best successes. They won the vote for women, helped to end apartheid, defeated the poll tax – all these courageous things – but now it feels like these movements are just afraid of doing anything new, anything that doesn't have a formal process. If you suggest something they've done ten million times they'll support it, but if you suggest something that's different, that doesn't fit their tick box, they'll throw it out.

As we explored earlier, the best learning doesn't come from listening only to your own side. Creating an open politics is about the challenge of difference. So my conversations also explored whether or not parties could work more closely together across party boundaries – not always or necessarily to agree, but to explore. In some ways the Coalition is living example of cross-party working, and, while there is antagonism and anger between the two ruling parties, there have also been some notable agreements. In Europe, of course, where coalition government is the norm, it is far more likely that parties will work together. Even here, they work together more than we think, and several of my interviewees talked about cross-party campaigns and meetings. As Ruth Lister points out, 'politicians and activists have always worked together to get things to happen'. And she also talks about moments when 'women across the house have come together on certain issues and the issues have transcended their political parties'. In her experience this happens more in the House of Lords, which is still tribal, but softened by the cross-benchers.

As Purna Sen says: 'Behind the scenes parties talk to each other – and are having to think about making accommodations across tribal boundaries that would once have been unthinkable.'

All politicians balance party allegiances with loose coalition and alliance work. But it isn't acknowledged, or praised, or demanded enough. For Natalie Bennett, there were two ways that parties could work together:

> in the world of ideas, and in campaigns. It's important in a cross-party context to try to be generous, not to attack someone because in your view their approach doesn't go far enough.

Of course for the Green Party:

> The big problem is that, because we have a first-past-the-post system, we have these scarring contests, where we throw everything at each other ... In continental Europe parties have to acknowledge that the person they're opposing may be someone that they'll be in coalition with in six months from now, whereas first-past-the-post encourages us to think of politics as a football match – I'm going to barge past everyone and get a goal in.

For citizens – who often support elements of one party's agenda and elements of another's – this working with people you don't always agree with is a matter of course. We see the theatre, the vitriol and the fake anger as childish. Natalie Bennett talked about the pettiness that could mar the effectiveness of politicians from minority parties. She mentioned one local authority where there is a single green councillor who can never find anyone to second her motions even when most of the council chamber agrees with her. So in our discussion we explored the need for greater generosity between the parties, and respect for the representative role of others.

IS THE DISTANCE FROM THE ELECTORATE TOO GREAT TO BRIDGE?

All my interviewees were passionate about changing their own political practice, and influencing others. But all acknowledged the scale of the 'disconnect' between politicians and the British public. The disconnect is worst among young people. Carys Afoko says:

> It's incredibly sad because politics has never been more important for my generation, we're saddled with student debt, we're trapped in expensive rented housing and unable to ever buy a home ... but fewer and fewer people get involved in party politics because of how detached it is from the realities of people's lives ...

Carys knows how unwelcoming the palace of Westminster can be for outsiders:

> The Westminster bubble can be quite lonely. I'm not sure if that is what everyone feels. I grew up in London, but Westminster feels like it must feel to live in a village – you just bump into the same people all the time. In the café there are the same people having the same conversations metres away from each other. The place closes in on itself. I find it a bit claustrophobic. You rarely get a sense that people in Westminster worry about how far away they are from other people's lives.

She tells a worrying story about working with young people:

I volunteer with a youth group, young people between about twelve and eighteen, and we did this project about human rights. We went away with them for a weekend and we went through the UN declaration of human rights and the rights of the child, and talked about what it meant, and found a language that made sense. The young people were really animated about injustice, and were emotional about how terrible human rights abuses were. But I found it a really sad conversation, because at the end they felt a sense of despair, a sense that there was nothing they could do, that nothing ever changes. They had absolutely no sense that anything they could do would make change happen.

What's even more worrying, she says, is that there is no sense of urgency about change …

And yet there are fewer and fewer people voting. I don't get it. If a company made a product that no-one was buying, they'd go out of business!

A Guardian poll in December 2013 showed that while 76 per cent of over-65s still voted, only 46 per cent of people aged 18 to 24 did so. This disconnect is not driven by apathy or boredom, but by anger – 47 per cent were angry, because governments didn't keep their promises, and didn't say what they believed.[1] Without a real, honest conversation, without a return to the complexity of human endeavour, politics is finished. Of course the public don't believe the sound bites: they are simplistic and puerile.

But some politicians are rebelling against the idea of politics as corporate marketing, breaking away from the 'script' dictated from the centre. Says Lisa Nandy:

We've got to see politicians loosen up, and to recognise that in this day and age it just doesn't work to have one message drilled into every member of a party for them to repeat. It can't work in an era when we're constantly accessible to people.

She is determined to challenge the language that politicians use:

We need to be seen as human, talking a language that people understand ... otherwise it turns people off. It's not boring just for young people. It's boring for everyone.

She feels it is important for politicians to stop spouting answers, and to be able to say 'that's interesting, tell me some more, what do you think the problem is? – how could we address it?', rather than treating every question as an excuse for a speech:

> Politicians need to be able to say 'I don't know'. Not, I haven't got a clue, but I've been thinking about this and it's really difficult. People do respond if you say it's complicated. When I'm talking to young people I say, you have to realise that if we scrap tuition fees it will cost a lot of money, and there will be a lot less money for other things. That's where the debate comes alive – when people level with each other and ask the real questions. Once you say this is what I want to do in principle, but I don't know how to do it, then there can be a real enquiry – a shared conversation ...

Jon Cruddas questioned whether the solutions to Labour's renewal would be found within the party:

> We need to start breathing again and loosen up and engage with more vibrant initiatives in civil society. Top-down command and control chokes off learning and exploration ... we need to become interested in the debates in other social movements, other political parties, other social democratic economies.

It would help if we could see politicians thinking and debating freely. The party conference circuit used to be a place where we could see what the big party debates were. It is depressing to realise that, in the UK at least, public debate has become less sophisticated than the private and informal conversations of everyday life. After all, we choose our politicians, ostensibly, for their ability to think and articulate ideas, for their political skill and experience – but then somehow the political process prevents them from sharing any of that with us.

One of the possibilities for a connection to younger people is, of course, social media. Lisa Nandy talked about having conversations with people on Twitter about possible solutions to social problems. Indra Adnan talks about the difference between the political response to Syria and Iraq being the real-time Twitter exchanges between MPs and their constituents.[2] For Lisa Nandy what is most crucial is to give voice to young people:

> Young people are deeply political, and have really really strong views, but they don't have a voice. They care passionately. They haven't switched off. They are engaged, but they don't know how to do it. We need to give them the tools to do it, not just through the schools but by giving people real power to exercise. The thing that troubles me most is that lots of young people who are political and have political views, but don't know that they do; or if they do, they don't know where to go with them and don't know how to exercise them. They feel that there isn't anywhere to influence real power. One thing we could do really quickly is to devolve real power to young people, enable young people to see that they're making an impact on their local communities. Once you've seen you're making an impact, you might get the confidence to make a leap into national politics. It's also about how we select young people for panels, and how we think about who we are consulting. We often ask the same people, but we should try to find young people for whom this is new. Young people who look at the system and say 'my god why would I ever do that'. They're the ones we need. The danger is that the only young people who come to Westminster to meet MPs are those who want to be part of it. I want to see the ones who say 'never in a million years', the ones who think it's completely broken.

Carys Afoko talks about the ways in which some political parties treat outsiders who are trying to join:

> Political parties don't invest enough in people, we don't look after the people in our local groups, we don't try to build confidence. People who want to change things aren't always welcome.

Instead of seeing new people as assets they are sometimes seen as potential problems or trouble-makers. They might want things to be done differently! We could be much more demo-cratic, more exciting and creative, but in reality, the most exciting and rewarding things I've done in politics have been in community groups ...

Some parties are trying to address this. Natalie Bennett talked about the early experiments of the Green Party, when they refused to have a leader and conducted meetings with a 'listening stick' so that ordinary members could be heard. But, she says:

We found that that can get quite tribal and rituals can be quite threatening.

The Greens have continued to lead the way in trying to change the way politics is done. Some of the things Natalie mentions are:

making chairing more inclusive, and making sure lots of people are trained to chair meetings, listening carefully to everyone, paying attention to how we structure a room and create an open environment, and recognising that everyone has something to contribute.

POLITICS OUTSIDE WESTMINSTER IS ALIVE AND WELL

Of course, although support for political parties is shrinking fast, politics across our society is alive and well. As Lisa Nandy says:

People are taking to the streets over tuition fees, austerity, cuts in benefits for people with disabilities. The occupy movement and lots of other groups are springing up in protest. It's not just about single issues, but about a broader set of values that people want to see reflected in the political debate.

There are thousands of NGOs and membership organisations that are testimony to our passion and sense of cause, from the Ramblers

to the Royal Society for the Protection of Birds, to UK Uncut and
the Save Our NHS party.

Many more of us are involved in active representative roles
than you would think. Alongside the sixty or so councillors in
every district or unitary council there are hundreds of school
governors, NHS governors, charitable committee members,
housing associations board members, sports clubs, etc. Many of
us volunteer, sign petitions, take civic action, go on demonstrations, hand out leaflets, write to the papers, take part in debates
on Facebook or Twitter. Young people are often highly politically
active but sceptical about political parties. A recent Guardian poll
found that young people felt it was more important to be heard
and to take a stand than to vote. We forget that the mass membership political party is a relatively recent phenomenon. The current
parties began as electoral coalitions in an embryonic democracy.
For many years the Liberals were the centre of a loose alliance of
causes and movements. The Labour Representation Committee,
when it was founded in 1900, was a coalition of trades unions,
the Fabians, the Independent Labour Party and the SDF, and the
Labour Party has remained federal in its structure to this day. The
union block vote is what is left of what was once a network of
organisations in civil society, combining together to maximise
votes for the causes they represented.

Political activity includes petitions, direct action and demonstrations; but most of it is about conversation, or debate, about
listening, talking, testing out ideas, persuading others. Politics is
the process through which identities and alliances are created.
Politics is about building consent, and shared interests, persuading
people whose lives are very different that they have enough
common cause to work together. It is a process of creating a shared
story that enables people to combine – to pull together, to compromise. It is the very process of creating 'the open tribe'. But even
here, says Rosie Rogers, there is far more that could be done:

> The problem is egos and silos: individual egos from people who
> don't want to listen to each other; and organisational egos
> where all they care about is the funding and the brand. If we

really wanted change, funders wouldn't make NGOs fight for the same funding. We would share more. NGOs and campaigning organisations would learn from each other. We would bring NGOs trying to do the same things together, and we would all work from offices in the same buildings and speak to each other and learn from each other. We'd have second-ments to each other's organisations to share ideas and do things to break down the silos. We would do more to live our values. We wouldn't exploit our workers. We would treat each other as we want to be treated.

In Chapter Seven we will explore some of the implications of a shift to networks and alliances. We still need political parties, since they provide the discipline and power to get people elected, but perhaps we are unlikely to recreate mass membership parties. The more interesting question is therefore whether political parties are able once again to look outwards to these broader alliances of people and organisations, with many shared perspectives and values. Can political parties – independently or in alliance – begin to see themselves simply as the hub of something much wider, and take responsibility not simply for their very narrow membership, but for the connections and linkages that go far beyond their formal edges – to the far wider group of people who share their values, and are willing to explore ideas?

POLITICS AS ENQUIRY

We have already explored the extent to which the open tribe is about balancing belonging and exploration – and it seems as if this process is perhaps at its most important in the world of politics. Could the principles we have been exploring offer a solution to the disconnect between the public and politicians? Is what we need to do to start a conversation?

In my conversation with Victor Adebowale I ask 'what would a politics be like that would bring people to complexity?' His response is that 'it starts with assuming that people will be inter-ested in discovery'. Victor's view is that true enquiry is a serious business of investigating exactly what are the real problems and what are the causes. 'Take the question of immigration', he says:

> Instead of assuming that immigration is a problem, or assuming that people are racist if they even raise the issue, let's explore it properly. Most economists believe that we need immigration – we need to attract the best brains from around the world. Most people understand that, so if there are genuine difficulties, say around housing or schools, we need to think about it together, and then have a conversation. It's the difference between proselytising and enquiry. We need a debate about how, if we need immigration, we get it to work, how additional people will fit in, for example. If the problem is housing, then we have to provide housing, and the question is then how do we do that? In the past housing was provided by the major employers who realised that it wasn't sensible to have a workforce that couldn't live in the city. Should we restart a conversation with employers about what their role is? Most people can talk about immigration rationally, and their concerns in a recession might well be about limited resources, so let's explore that. People feel 'my job's at risk' – is it, from whom? Which jobs are at risk? Why? It helps to be specific. Those people who have practical knowledge and experience should be able to share it, so that we can find, and solve, the real problems. Politics usually deals with the perception, not the problem, and so responds to the perception but leaves the problem. We need to treat people as adults – here are the facts, these are some of the assumptions, let's explore how true they are.

He went on to give the example of northern European migrants picking cabbages in Lincolnshire:

> If we want cabbages, and they need to be picked, someone has to pick them. And if British workers, and even British teenagers, find the work too repetitive, to dull, too poorly paid, we need to think about what that means. If people are coming here to take on roles we don't want to take on, we need to explore that. It's a

conversation about the shape of the economy, it's a conversation worth having ...

And as Victor says, there's something about enquiry which is specific. It means not stopping at generalisations. He argues that the reason so many government policies fail is that they are not the result of careful analysis and discussion – they originated with a sound bite.

Carys Afoko talks about needing to take people's fears seriously:

> We need to acknowledge people's fears and recognise that they're not just being racist. We can't win without understanding why people feel the way they do. We need to find a way to talk about this that acknowledges people's fears. They experience politicians as not really listening, just saying that they're wrong. We need to start where people are, even if it's factually inaccurate. People are not stupid – their concerns are not without foundation, they are responding to their own experience. Listening should be the start of all our politics, because people's concerns don't come from nowhere – if people can't get a flat, then that might be because there are not enough flats! Nigel Farage is winning support because he is saying people have a right to be heard ...

Ironically, behind closed doors, in our homes, in the private conversations of politicians, far more sophisticated conversations are going on – and compromises are being made, people are learning to change their views in debate. As Lisa Nandy says:

> Wouldn't it be great if we could have those conversations out in the open so that people could understand that we know things are complicated?

Could we begin to think differently about the process of politics itself? Instead of seeing it, in Jon Cruddas's phrase, 'as the transmission of the fixed answer', could we see it as a process of enquiry? In Chapter Six we explore the scope for collaborative, civic enquiry, a place where we, as citizens, explore how to resolve the difficult questions of our day, and, through doing so, come up with suffi-cient, temporary answers to enable us to move forward. This is Victor Adebowale's idea of progression – a slow process of social evolution that enables civil society to survive new challenges.

NOTES

1. ICM poll, Guardian, 27.12.13.
2. Indra Adnan, 'New Times change happens when you are not looking', Compass website, 18.11.13.

4. On the side of the people not the machine

In my conversation with Ruth Lister, one of the most important anti-poverty campaigners of the past fifty years, she began by discussing the nature of work:

> I am always concerned about the dreadful quality of some of the work that's on offer. There are often really low wages for what is arduous drudgery, with no control over the work-process, long hours doing menial tasks with little or no control over the work-process – work that doesn't respect or involve people's full humanity.

Ruth was questioning the 'fetishism of work, under both New Labour and the Tories, the assumption that we should all be in paid work, at all costs, regardless of the quality of the work or the rewards of the work'.

In the introduction we discussed the idea of the open tribe seeking a balance between the desires we have to explore, create and challenge, and the need we have to feel safe, and connected, and to be protected from harm. Since work is such an important part of our lives, it should be a place where this tension is played out, and a good balance found. Paid work has, through the centuries, offered a way out of closed communities, an escape from the home, a chance to see the world. At its best, work is a territory of adventure and self-discovery, a place where we achieve proficiency, and even mastery, a way of proving ourselves, and of demonstrating our value to others. Instead, for many of us work is either exploitative and degrading, or stressful and frightening. How did we get to here?

WHAT HAVE WE DONE TO WORK?

Work can be extraordinarily fulfilling. It can offer a daily test of ingenuity and skill, of our intelligence and problem-solving, and our ability to learn and improve. Work, at its best, is a social place, where people come together to perform tasks in teams and to collaborate to achieve a worthwhile goal. Work can be a congenial place to meet friends and create solidarity based on shared experience and shared endeavour. Work is also, especially for women, a place where we can escape the grind of unpaid domestic labour, and discover a wider world of difference, of diversity, of new and different tastes and smells and sounds, where we can learn new skills and discover things about ourselves – a source of liberation from the narrow confines and assumptions of family. In the nineteenth and early twentieth centuries, factory and office work for women offered a new freedom; women able to earn their own money were no longer dependent on fathers or husbands for survival.

Mental work can be creative, imaginative and thought-provoking. Manual work enables us to test out boundaries and use our strength, releasing tension and creating a happy exhaustion. Mastery of a craft that enables us to create something beautiful or useful, as Sennett so brilliantly describes in his book *Craftwork*, is a source of inherent satisfaction.[1]

So what have we done to work, to make it so often stressful, exploitative and de-humanising? During the industrial revolution, Karl Marx and other social commentators wrote in horror at the dehumanisation that accompanied the move to vast mills and factories, and about the loss of skill and autonomy that accompanied the death of hand crafted manufacture.

Marx described as 'alienation' the process whereby a waged worker was separated from control over their labour, no longer able to make choices or judgements, treated simply as a component in a vast machine. He drew attention to the dehumanising impact of a working life where, for the hours people are at work, they sell themselves into temporary slavery – forced to hand over control over their bodies and minds, unable to think for themselves or to use their creativity and imagination. A key element of alienation, for Marx, was alienation from what he called *gattungswesen* – species essence or human potential.[2] We are psychically damaged if we are not able to see our work as meaningful and purposeful. Our human potential can only be achieved at work if we are able to direct our actions towards demands we have placed upon ourselves, rather than demands placed upon us by others. Marx was talking primarily about factory workers. He would have been horrified to discover that in transferring factory-based systems to offices and to the public sector, we have extended alienation to white collar workers and to professionals, creating 'factory conditions' for call-centre workers, social workers, teachers, nurses.

An unintended side effect of the introduction of performance management into public services has been the loss of a sense of vocation, and the shift from personal responsibility as an autonomous professional to being part of a system. Tom Jackson argues that we should challenge the idea that higher productivity is always good.[3] There are some jobs where working faster makes no sense at all. The quality of work if you are a teacher, a carer, a social worker, a psychiatrist, a musician, depends not on producing more per hour of labour, but on the amount of time you lavish on a relationship with a person, or on mastering a task proficiently. In many areas of work to speed up is to become less effective, less kind, less proficient, less safe. Toby Lowe argues that the current trend towards payment by results can only worsen the effect. Payment by results undermines workers ability to respond flexibly to complex situations and treats every situation with the same 'intervention', regardless of the differences between people:

> payment by results does not reward organisations for supporting people to achieve what they need, it rewards organisations for producing data about targets; it rewards organisations for the fictions their staff are able to invent about what they have achieved.[4]

Loew argues that it makes people dishonest who would otherwise have wanted to work with integrity. How can staff admit that their work is not effective, and explore the reasons why, if they will lose business, or perhaps their jobs, as a result? Gwyn Bevan at LSE and Christopher Hood at Oxford have concluded that results targets in the NHS always create gaming.[5]

One of the results of the unprecedented cuts in public services since 2010 is that for some public sector staff work has become frightening. I often act as an executive coach to quite senior public sector managers, and since 2010 I have been really alarmed at the number of senior, skilled, professionals who come to coaching sessions in tears, or with levels of stress that are close to illness – people who are working fourteen-hour days and are unable to get through the work; people frightened about the impact that cuts will have on vulnerable service users; dealing with the moral dilemmas of unsafe levels of staffing and impossible demands. In parts of the private sector, where rewards are often dispropor-tionate, high flyers can nevertheless be expected to work twenty-hour days, or be fired at a moment's notice – and carry dangerous levels of stress and fear. If work is stressful at the top, what on earth is it like at the bottom?

Ruth Lister says:

> I like the ILO concept of decent work and we should be talking more about that – talking about decent work, decent wages. I prefer decent wages and decent conditions to the concept of a living wage. And the thing that matters most to people is having some sort of control over your work environment, your working day.

She points out that health research has shown that that what causes much poor health is the sense of powerlessness at work. As she also points out, changing this doesn't necessarily cost money.

LOW PAY

One of the things that makes work intolerable is low pay. Low pay is a crucial determinant of poverty. And despite the growing affluence of our society, average earnings have been falling in real terms across the UK. Real wages have fallen since 2010, and, despite real economic growth between 2003 and 2008, workers at median pay levels and below experienced wages that were flat or falling in real terms. Those at the bottom have faced the greatest reductions, and increasing numbers are falling below the relative low pay threshold of earning less than two thirds of gross hourly median pay. The numbers of people defined as earning less than a living wage has risen sharply from 3.4 million to 4.8 million.[6] Poverty is no longer about unemployment. Most of those paid less than £7 an hour are part-time, the majority are women. Many are working fewer hours than they would like to – and we don't yet know how many people are locked into zero hours contracts. According to Julia Unwin of the Joseph Rowntree Foundation, 'the most distinctive characteristic of poverty today is the very high number of working people who are also poor'.[7]

The average full-time British worker puts in 42.7 hours a week, the longest working week in Europe, and even that, for many, is not enough to meet basic needs. Almost a third of families with children living in poverty are couples with a single breadwinner.[8] Wages that are too low mean that people can't live on them without taking two jobs, or doing overtime, without both parents returning to work when their children are still too small, without extra jobs on the side – without parents doing alternate night and day shifts so that they never meet. If wages are too low, people have no chance of a good life. And wages are not low because we live in a poor society. We have broken the link between productivity and wages. A greater and greater proportion of GDP is now going to profits. As average wages fall, the wealthy are getting wealthier.

Nor is it true that there is a gulf between 'hard-working families' and scroungers – one in six of the economically active population has claimed job seekers allowance at least once in the past two years – the majority claiming for less than six months. 33 per cent of people experienced low income levels at least once over a four-year period.[9] For a significant proportion of the population just getting by is stressful. And it's not as if low wages for the very poorest workers benefits the vast majority of us. Low wages in the modern welfare state mean that the taxpayer is always subsidising the capitalist. The numbers of working people claiming tax credits has risen 50 per cent since 2003 – to 3.3 million in 2012. Vast profits can be made by private companies because wages are subsidised by tax credits and benefits. Our taxes are subsidising the profits of companies. And then to add insult to injury, some major companies evade, or avoid the tax they owe to maximise profits – which is really simply stealing from the people. Governments, by letting these things happen, penalise good and responsible employers and reward the greedy.

For a growing number of workers, often young, often migrant, wages are falling; zero hours contracts remove any job security, control is non-existent; participation in decision making has disappeared. Work isn't fun any more. The factory acts were passed in the nineteenth century to prevent the worst excesses of exploitation – child labour, endless working days, dangerous shifts. In the twentieth century, health and safety and the minimum wage continued to extend protection to those who could not protect themselves. In the name of 'deregulation' we are turning the clock back, and re-creating a chasm between the work 'haves' and 'have-nots'.

Many of the poorest paid are in the hospitality industries, in hotels and restaurants. But perhaps saddest of all is the growing army of poorly paid carers. We have managed to create a sense that caring, for the elderly, for the vulnerable, for those least able to help themselves, has become a valueless, exploited, unrecognised calling. Much of this care is done without wages, by frail partners and exhausted daughters or sisters. But even when care is provided by the state, the carers are hired as cheap, poorly trained labour by private companies or voluntary organisations. Since commissioners have been forced to push down prices, carers for older people on zero hours contracts 'clock in' to a frail older person's home using an electronic diary, and are then timed: they may be allowed seven minutes or fifteen, to complete all the tasks that old person needs, and will be penalised if they take longer than the allotted time. It leads to nasty choices – shall they prioritise taking their charge to the toilet, or giving them breakfast? Washing them, or attending to the telephone calls beeping on the answer-phone? Clearing up a mess, or cleaning their teeth? Management, somewhere in a distant building, are monitoring the electronic diaries, and setting the rules.

A few years ago, my brother, who is severely disabled, was confronted not by the carer he had grown used to and recognised, but by an unannounced stranger. He found it disturbing and upsetting. Later a letter arrived to say that all the carers had been rotated, because they had been discovered 'forming relationships' with clients. Further investigation revealed that nothing sinister had happened; the relationships in question were friendships, and, through kindness, the paid carers had been going out of their way to do extra little helpful jobs or pop to the shops, thus spending more time than had been allotted and failing to meet their targets.

To work ten hours a day (since travel time between clients is unpaid) for less than the minimum wage, doing difficult work with very ill or very frail people, with poor supervision, but tight control – especially for a young person newly arrived in this country – must be stressful, scary and dangerous. And yet, caring ought to be one of the most important things we do.

Who is the 'we' that can't afford decent working conditions? Levels of inequality now match those in Edwardian times, and authors like Stewart Lansley argue cogently that high levels of inequality make our overall economic success worse, not better.[10] Some people are getting very rich because the rest of us have accepted that we should get poorer. Some people are living wasteful, spendthrift lives, because others have no alternative but drudgery. In 1945, people who had fought against fascism during the war were determined to change what they saw as unacceptable inequality and so the welfare state was inaugurated. But in the twenty-first century the gains that were made then are being increasingly eroded.

If we are to become again one society – an open tribe – then we have to think very carefully about the level of unequal work that can be tolerated. Somehow, on both the right and the left we have created an image of our economy as an inexorable force, capable of twisting humans to its ends, capable of destroying human relationships and over-running human concerns. This sort of thinking lets politicians and the wealthy off the hook. It isn't capitalism that decides whether children should labour in third world factories, or women in Bangladesh work in unsafe buildings, whether profits should be made from people's addictions and insecurities, whether wages should be driven below what is needed to survive, whether training should be abandoned and lunch breaks abolished. Capitalism is, at core, a human system. The rules we have evolved have been designed to create wealth for some people and not for others. They could be designed differently.

Nor is there one single capitalism; there are many sorts. We are capable, as societies, of choosing between them, and of enforcing ethics and behaviours that remove the worst excesses we currently experience. We could begin to demand, as a society, the ethics and behaviours that go alongside a sustainable system, and to name the values that ought to be followed. We could demand – as citizens and as consumers – that companies act within an ethical, socially responsible framework. We have already begun to withdraw our custom from companies that exploit workers or children in the third world. In my conversation with David Marquand he talked about the different rules that apply in Germany and in other Scandinavian countries. All systems have their downsides as well as their upsides, but in those countries locally responsible firms, regional banks and manufacturing companies connected to their local communities all demonstrate a market economy capable of working within decent, life-affirming rules. Wealth creation is not necessarily cruel. Indeed, employee-owned firms such as John Lewis, large-scale co-operatives such as Mondragon, Fair Trade companies, successful public sector trading companies such as East Coast Mainline, all show how different values can lead to successful enterprise.

We are encouraged by the red-top newspapers and some politicians to be fearful about immigrants and foreigners coming to take our jobs, accepting lower rates of pay and poorer working conditions. But instead of penalising those workers, we could protect them, insist on minimum living wages, on maximum working hours, on decent working conditions. We have the regulatory frameworks, we have the power. We could ask more of business. But even current regulations are not properly enforced. The fines for not paying the minimum wage are lower than the fines for fly-tipping.

THERE'S MORE TO LIFE THAN WORK

Ruth Lister talked about the ambivalence that many women feel about paid work. Those of us with our roots in feminism saw paid work as hugely important to open up opportunities for women. The companionship and sense of identity women gained, even in relatively menial work, were a vital counterweight to the often confining private sphere of the home. But women still bear the lion's share of domestic responsibilities, and without decent free childcare or any comprehensive support for the elderly, women have paid a high price for their entry into the labour force. Women still are mostly responsible for the care of children, and for elderly parents, and yet we make very little allowance for this in our assumptions that 'everyone' should have paid work.

For men also, the dominance of work over their whole lives is neither healthy nor, in the end, desired. A palliative nurse has recently been conducting interviews with the dying, asking if they have any regrets. Almost unanimously, the men interviewed said they regretted how hard they'd worked, and what they had lost in terms of relationships and family life.

Ruth Lister said we should pay more attention to the relationship between work and other activities:

> I would like to see a shorter working week. I would like to see a better balance between the paid work that men and women do, to enable men to make more of a contribution in the home. I would like everyone to have more time for other things, be it politics or civic things or just having fun, just being. I think the politics of time is an important part of the good society, and while, of course, paid work has to be done, we have to make sure

it's shared out fairly so we don't have some people working very long hours while others can't get work. We need to put work in its place and not treat it as the be all and end all ... Those of us who love our work, for whom it isn't at all alienating, can still end up working too long hours and it's a real trap – one that I've fallen into – but there is more to life than work.

John Maynard Keynes famously predicted in 1930 that technological change would mean that by the twenty-first century no-one would need to work more than fifteen hours a week. Instead, we have chosen to consume more, buy bigger cars, more furniture, convenience foods, labour saving devices, gadgets, foreign holidays – so that these things all become normal, expected, necessary. But need it be like this? There is an exciting movement growing now to reduce working hours. In *Time on Our Side*, Anna Coote writes: 'suppose we did paid work for 30 instead of 40 hours a week?', and asks how we could 'change our habits of thought and practice, our regulations and institutions to build a new consensus about what makes a "normal" paid working week'.[11] Valerie Bryson suggests that if we created shorter working hours we would automatically make gender equality more likely and begin to value patterns of time use that are more typically female.[12] We would have time for more than just work and child-care, we would begin to see caring as an enjoyable activity – instead of hustling up enough childcare to cope with long hours at work, we would have time to be with our kids.

And an important by-product of more time would be the space to think, to consider our lives and our surroundings, to get involved in local activities, to volunteer, to join local groups and clubs, to garden, take photographs, make music, take part in amateur dramatics. And the more time we have, the easier we will find it to make friends, to look after neighbours, to be curious about the people who live in our street, to make connections, to talk. Time is an important dimension if we are to connect up our open tribes.

The solution to working too hard depends on the reason for it. For the very poorest, who are forced to work long hours simply to survive, the answer is to pay more. As a society, we need to ensure that full-time, paid work with reasonable hours pays sufficiently well to raise a family, and have a decent life. For rich workaholics, or for the lonely with no other life than work, the answer to working too hard is more difficult. We need to rethink how we value and reward over-working, to treat it as a cause for concern rather than something to brag about.

Victor Adebowale argued that everyone should have an opportunity to have a balanced life – and particularly a life balanced between work and the rest of our responsibilities. People suffer when they are forced into unbalance. For him, work should offer respect, wisdom and love:

> People I find are most ill at ease – regardless of their income and wealth – when they have a life that is unbalanced, being forced into a single track, either because of your psychological make-up or because you are driven by outside forces. The good life is one where you have the ability and privilege to balance your different wants and needs and are allowed to live in ordinary unhappiness with dignity.

BEING HUMAN AT WORK

But we need to go further. It's not enough just to be unhappy at work for fewer hours. If we are to become an open tribe, we also need to think about how we make being at work a different sort of experience. We need to find ways to make work pleasurable – not simply for the lucky few high flyers, but for most of us. Much of what makes work pleasurable is not the work itself, but the relationships with colleagues and the way we are treated. Work is crucially a place where we meet people different from ourselves – people from other tribes, from whom we could learn. There is something vital about being able to bring our whole human capability to work, and to find ways to make it rewarding, either through the relationships we form, or the control we have over the things we make or what we learn. When we're at work, we want to be treated with respect, to be consulted, to be given opportunities to use our full humanity – and not treated as a component of a machine.

The movement 'More Like People' is about trying to create a more human experience at work. They are keen to explore ways to break down barriers at work that get in the way of relationships. They argue that hierarchical decision-making reduces trust and responsibility: that rigid standards of professional behaviour make it near impossible for people to be themselves; and teams, departments and job titles keep us from following our passions, our interests and our strengths, forcing us to underperform in roles that don't bend to the complexity of what we are dealing with, or don't respond to the simple human changes in mood which mean we'd be better off doing different work on a given day. They ask difficult questions like, 'how could we let individual passion and energy dictate the flow of our work?' and 'how could our work incorporate more than the practical tasks, and offer a place to share stories, bring our families, get to know each other?'[13]

These ideas were echoed in my interview with Willie Sullivan:

I don't understand why in the twenty-first century we can't pay everyone a decent wage and make work interesting. Our idea of the good life has changed and it's no longer simply about basic amenities – central heating and inside toilets – now it's becoming more important to have meaning in our lives. Even the most repetitive jobs can be made interesting through good relationships, or by having control over the way you organise your work, by giving people skills and encouraging them to use them. I can't see why, for people who make coffee, employers can't make the social aspect of the job rewarding. That's been my realisation. Not everyone can work in think-tanks, but people find meaning in different things, and work is such an important part of our lives, we have to find meaning there too. It's not as difficult as it sounds. I was reading the other day about the difference between the German labour market and the English labour market. If you're a shop assistant in Germany, they give you control over your work area, so you have to plan it and organise it, and because of that responsibility you are paid more – whereas here we divide work up into meaningless tasks with no real control or power to make a difference, so that we can pay people less and less … creating jobs with no meaning.

The 1970s movement for workplace democracy has all but died away. Now we leave it to individual corporations to enthuse their staff, and treat them well only if they so choose. And yet employee-owned organisations that engage and involve their staff in decision-making tend to out perform conventional organisations. All the management textbooks and leadership manuals talk about empowering and engaging staff, about culture change and encouraging creativity, but many workplaces, in both private and public sectors, fall back on good old command and control. Psychologists report an increase in micro-management and a culture of blame as adding to workplace stress.[14] It's hard to judge what is lost in terms of productivity when staff are disengaged, frightened or depressed. But it's easy to measure in human terms. Mental illness is rising rapidly – and studies increasingly identify the experience of work as an important component of mental health.[15] The quality of relationships at work, the extent to which we are able to grow, our sense of our own identity and worth, all these things are part of what makes us fully human at work.

In those jobs that involve service to the public, in either the private or public sector, those relationships are not simply with bosses, but with members of the public. Victor Adebowale tells the story about being a road-sweeper in Wakefield:

It taught me a lot. For some rich people, workers at the bottom of the pile are not colleagues or fellow citizens, or members of the same tribe helping each other by fulfilling different tasks – but servants – or less … I observed that some people treated me literally as expendable, as a non-person. Others treated me with a kind of confused respect. They wanted to respect me but I was a road sweeper. Others just saw me as a human being, and were intrigued, and got into conversation with me. And of course I wanted to be treated like that – as a human being. The opposite of that is that you are slotted in, a unit, a functionary whose only role is to give something to someone else who you have never met, and who doesn't care about you, to produce money for them, or to service them. And I think the human condition rejects that.

Victor talks about society needing to progress:

Progression is a society in which every individual treats every other individual as a human being, with wisdom, with wonder and with love. And where the structures we create pursue that aim. That's progression. The opposite of that is a society where you are slotted, you are a unit.

He made me reflect on my own behaviour when I am tired, or stressed. If we ignore waiters, walk past toilet attendants, or are rude to airport workers when planes are delayed, we collude with the assumption that these people are less than our equals. Manners, empathy, good behaviour are part of an open tribe – and as customers we can have an impact on the lived experience of others at work.

A DIFFERENT SORT OF WORK

Theodore Zeldin asks whether we can invent jobs to suit people, instead of making people behave in ways that suit the machinery or the bureaucratic process.[16] In Renaissance times, work for the lucky few could offer a rich combination of farming, diplomacy, engineering, craft and artistic endeavour, all mixed up together. Even for the poorest peasants, work involved considerable complexity, and a lot of different activities. Do we really believe in the twenty-first century that treating human beings as if they are components in a vast computer or machine is productive? If a task is machine-like, it can probably nowadays be done by a machine. Humans should begin to concentrate their efforts on bringing the full creativity of the human spirit to endeavour – solving problems, building understanding, creating relationships, using their full intellectual capacity.

It is telling that the younger generation is rejecting manual labour and repetitive, humdrum, over-controlled, work. My generation's standard response is to worry about their lack of work ethic, the unreality of their aspirations and to complain of the laziness of 'the X-factor generation'. But actually, given the quality of the technology we are evolving, are they being unrealistic? Why is work so dull? So dispiriting? Surely in the twenty-first century workers deserve better? Zeldin asks whether we over-specialise – whether we are too ready to abandon a liberal arts education that equips us 'for anything':

> Something new is needed, for students, managers and employees alike, for all those who sense that their mental processes are beginning to go rigid and want to make a last bid to remain free, who are not content to be just professionals and who want jobs that make them better people.[16]

Zeldin argues that conversations, good ones, might be alternative ways of learning to conventional, highly specialised 'teaching'.

What if we didn't simply do one job all the time, but several jobs one day a week – or a job that combined many different elements? What if the nature of work was to change entirely – so that we combined some professional work, with some manual labour, with something creative? What if we stopped thinking about working in a single 'job' altogether? We need to think some more about how break out of being treated like bits of a machine.

Maybe we should not try to separate out our 'work selves' from our 'real selves', stop allowing our work to define us, or others. Perhaps social relationships would begin to change if we didn't think of ourselves as 'our jobs' but as more complex people undertaking a range of activities. Perhaps it would be more difficult to dismiss someone as 'just a cleaner' or 'a boring suit' if we knew they only did that for a third of their time. What if we took portfolio careers a stage further – and began to routinely do more than one job, with very different characteristics? I know of an accountant who gave that work up to retrain as a skilled carpenter, but despite years of making furniture of extraordinary beauty, was unable to make ends meet, and is returning to accountancy. But what if she didn't have to choose? What if it became a standard thing to do accountancy three days a week and carpentry for two? We know that out-of work actors are also waiters and baristas; that consultant geriatricians are also saxophone players. Ironically, this 'more than one job' life is often only available for the very rich and the very poor. But what if it became normal? What if the voluntary activity, or the poorly paid creative work that we do for love, became more of who we were? What if we stopped valuing 'specialisation' and thought more highly of a training that allowed people to work holistically, doing whatever was needed – being teachers and police officers, or social workers and mental health specialists, nurses and speech therapists? What if we reversed the past fifty years, and returned to deeper, wider professional training, where we learn to see the whole person, not simply a disease, or a condition.

What if the open tribe begins to redefine what work is, and begins to recombine mental and physical labour, closing the gap between 'brain' workers and 'manual workers: if we begin to celebrate craft skills as well as artistic intention, execution rather than simply management? Perhaps we could go back to a world where engineers are also poets, and the clergy are also botanists.

Creating an open tribe at work would mean redrawing the balance between entrepreneurialism and 'command and control' – creating scope for innovation throughout organisations, not just at the top, while sharing some of the difficult decision-making that lands on the shoulders of the bosses. We would learn from each other, treating the rich talk of an organisation as a source of learning and growth – making space for ideas to grow and for leadership to take place at all levels. We would see challenge and difference as a source of new ideas. We would be constantly searching for learning from elsewhere, while honouring the commitment and energy from within. We would respect the calling people have towards compassion and excellence, and reward it. We would recreate a life-enhancing balance between work and leisure and family. And we would pay ourselves enough, so that if we worked full-time we could afford to look after our families without depending on the state.

NOTES

1. Richard Sennett, *The Craftsman*, Penguin, London 2009.
2. Karl Marx, *Economic and Philosophic Manuscripts*, 1844.
3. Tom Jackson, 'The Trouble with Productivity', in Anna Coote and Jane Franklin (eds), *Time on our Side*, NEF, London 2013.
4. Toby Lowe, 'Payment by Results', *Guardian*, 1.2.14.
5. Gwyn Bevan and Christopher Hood, 'What's measured is what matters: targets and gaming in the English public healthcare system', *Public Administration*, 2006 84 (3).
6. Defined as £7.20 an hour by academics at the Centre for Research in Social Poverty, and as £8.30 an hour in London.
7. Julia Unwin, Chief Executive of the Joseph Rowntree Foundation, quoted in press release of the launch of the JRF 2013 Poverty Report, written by the New Policy Institute.
8. JRF research by NatCen, 13.11.13.
9. JRF, *Annual Monitoring Poverty and Exclusion Report* (written by New Policy Institute) 2013.
10. See Stewart Lansley, *The Cost of Inequality; Why Economic Equality is Essential for Recovery*, Gibson Square, London 2011.
11. Anna Coote, 'A new economics of work and time', in *Time on our Side*.
12. Valerie Bryson, 'Time, care and gender inequalities', in *Time on our Side*.
13. See the More like People website
14. Catherine Quinn, 'Mind over Matter', *Guardian*, 20.1.09.
15. A study by the Mental Health Charity Mind in 2000 showed that of 1500 people interviewed, 61 per cent believed that work stress was the main cause of their problems (BBC News Report 10.10.00). An OECD study in 2011 reported that job insecurity and pressure in workplaces was driving a rise in mental illness across the OECD countries (*Sick on the Job: Myths and Realities about Mental Health at Work*, OECD, December 2011).
16. Theodore Zeldin, *Conversation*.

5. CAN THE STATE LOVE?

We cannot travel far along the road to the open tribe without encountering the role of the state. In previous chapters we have explored the idea of balancing the sense of belonging that comes from 'tribe' with the sense of openness which enables us to welcome and learn from strangers. We discussed the importance of connection, and of being fully human, at work and in all our relationships with others. The state is an important part of our connectedness with others, since it makes possible the provision of the resources that sustain many of the most important parts of our lives. We know that the way we are treated fundamentally affects how we behave to others: more and more of our encounters, in health, education, social care, welfare, employment, skills development, involve government. So how government behaves shapes our society. Schools are probably the most important foundation of our social selves, while the way we are treated in the health and social care system shapes our sense of our own worth. The state, by the way it interacts with citizens, reinforces the values that define a society. If the state is mean, ungenerous, suspicious and defensive, that begins to define the society within which we live.

Key to a sense of belonging are issues of citizenship and entitlement. Who is included? What happens to those people who are left out? In this fast moving global world, to be stateless is to be powerless. There is an increasingly vociferous clamour about entitlement and belonging, trying to make sure that foreigners, incomers, migrants, outsiders, don't gain access to 'our' hard-won resources. This is not new. In the 1960s local and central government set draconian residence qualifications, of up to ten years, before new arrivals were eligible for what was then seen as the most important public good, council housing. Of course in those days foreigners were as likely to be Irish, or from another part of England, as they were to be arrivals from the commonwealth or Eastern Europe. Today we are trying to police access to health services, and entitlements to benefits. Of course, it is entirely legitimate to enquire into the ways that benefits in a society are shared out, and what constitutes an entitlement to social goods. But we are silent about how much of our society's resources should be available for the social goods that protect against want and destitution. As social goods are cut back, and corporations and rich individuals avoid the tax that would have paid for them, there is an increasing clamour to exclude as many people as possible.

This is not simply about new arrivals or migration. The idea of a welfare safety net that protects everyone is also undermined by a new vocabulary about avoiding dependence and ensuring people 'earn' the right to the help and support they need. The language tries to separate 'hard-working families' from the others. It is not even any longer the age-old distinction between the 'deserving' and the 'undeserving' poor, since those that are seen as a drain on the work of others include people with disabilities, the old and the frail. To 'belong' to this narrowing, closed tribe, everyone has to stand on their own two feet. Instead of wanting to share good fortune, and use resources collaboratively, we are encouraged to feel cheated if our taxes go to help others. The new defensiveness defines everyone in need of help, who is struggling, who needs work, or a home or care, as 'not like us'.

Churchill famously said that a civilisation is judged by the way it treats prisoners. The state demonstrates the values of a society by the way it treats those that are at its mercy – imprisoned, dependent, vulnerable. Our society is defined by the way the state treats the old, the frail, children, youngsters, down-and-outs, the disabled, those who are mentally and physically ill, jobless, homeless. In a democracy, the state is expected to set the rules that condition our encounters with each other, and the values that underpin our social behaviour. And the rules set by the state always have the greatest impact on those who are most in need.

David Marquand helped me to think about the extent to which the British government has swallowed the idea of people as 'homo economicus' – measuring everything by its economic value, and seeing paid work as the only valuable activity. And this is even more disappointing when the state plays such a major part in what's left of our non-market economy: an economy in which other values could and should operate. The state historically has looked after and supported those unable to work and those left vulnerable by open markets, but it now seems determined to reinforce, rather than challenge, the logic of brute capitalism.

My conversation with Hilary Cottam took me furthest into an exploration of the role, or the potential role, that a different sort of state could play if we were to behave as an open tribe. Hilary is a social scientist and anthropologist now leading experiments supporting vulnerable older people and troubled families. She argues that the way the state provides support is fundamentally undermining of people's human capacity to grow and change. She argues that trying to keep people out of welfare, ironically, does the opposite: by seeing the offer of help as something that only happens as a 'last resort', we neglect and undermine the informal support networks within communities. Our insistence on standardised assessments of 'need' and professional judgements about disability, dysfunction and failure, means that we take no account of capability and strength:

> I've been working for a long time within public services and it strikes me how much of the state's resource is spent keeping people out of the system … we see up to 80 per cent of the resource being spent on processes to decide who gets in.

Hilary talks about the increase of process compliance and form filling, which means that the vast bulk of professionals' time – social workers, clinicians, district nurses – is spent in front of computers or in meetings with other professionals, rather than in interventions with the clients:

> More and more professionals are specialists who spend their time assessing people: so, for example, an educational psychologist may spend all their time giving a child a statement rather than

doing developmental work with that child. As resources shrink, I have seen the practical effects of concentrating on assessment – sometimes the only thing that the state provides is the assessment, and you are given a form that says what the problem is, but there is no resource left to do anything about it.

Her alternative, which she has been building through powerful demonstration projects, is to start with the strength and ambition of people who find themselves in difficult circumstances, and to provide the human, personal support that people need to find a life that will be satisfying whatever their disadvantages. Hilary has been involved from the beginning in setting up the Circle movement (www.circlecentral.com), a membership organisation that supports the 50+ age group to sustain strong social bonds and take care of their practical needs. Everyone contributes what they can to create a reinforcing circle of reciprocal help. Nottingham Circle, for example, provides a rich calendar of social events, and members and paid-for helpers provide practical support, such as someone able-bodied to change light-bulbs or take out heavy rubbish; but on top of the basic platform, people begin to build social and leisure networks – organising theatre parties in which people with physical disabilities are escorted by less frail neighbours, or dinner clubs in which old people cook and eat together.

> The challenges people face – poverty, lack of opportunity, mental health, parenting – these are universal problems. And the more people are in the solution, the stronger the solution will be. So how do we get more people in and build solutions that are rich and strong rather than moving to the defensive idea of keeping people out? What is important about social networks is that the more people use them the more they grow, and the more people are taking part and putting things onto a platform the more they use them, whether that's time or money. So this is a completely different way of looking at the world… instead of gate-keeping.

Hilary says we need to recognise and value people's capabilities and contribution, rather than seeing them as a cost. This chimes with me, because of my own involvement in a project called the 'Ageing Well' programme, funded by the Local Government Association, which piloted 'asset-based' approaches to improving the well-being of older people. In twenty localities around the country, the project brought older people together with voluntary sector projects, community organisations, professionals, the local council and the health service, to identify the existing resources and assets that could be better used for older people – their own resources, community assets, private sector assets, buildings, shops, cars, churches, parks. We produced maps, and amid much hilarity, generated scores of ideas for supper clubs, befriending groups, using pubs to replace dismal lunch clubs, creating exercise groups in parks, setting up voluntary community transport schemes, organising Pilates and dance classes in church halls. The older people were more creative and more energetic than most of the representatives of state agencies – and with the help of some creative volunteers and here and there an enthusiastic vicar, an enlightened director of social care, a third sector entrepreneur or a committed care-home worker – we began to create new services. These needed pump priming support from local councils or health organisations, but were run mostly from the assets and energy in civil society. As one table of feisty eighty year olds reported back at one event, 'you should go and visit the very frailest and isolated people, and instead of asking them what they need, you should ask them what they can contribute'. Because, as they made clear, it is by contributing to society, looking after others, making a difference, that we gain a sense of meaning and purpose to life, that we attain dignity and respect. Hilary describes the scope to build on this approach:

> These Circles have been proven to work, so why wouldn't the next government just scale this up across the country immediately? The value is that it becomes a self-perpetuating system – the more people join, the more other people join the more that can be offered … and then we can start a conversation. Circle does preventative work and low level social care, but could do so much more. We could begin to build more adult

services onto that platform, we could build on what we have done. But that rarely happens. What happens is that the rest of the system ignores what we have learnt and carries on, and meanwhile a paper is produced by a government department with a little box that describes Circle as 'good practice'. But unless you invest and begin to unlock resources and think about how this could be built on in other spheres, and other parts of the economy, we don't move it on.

Participle, the organisation that developed Circles, has been working not just with older people, but also with very troubled families, in radical approaches that go well beyond those adopted by conventional government schemes. These are important because they begin to move into the less comfortable territory of support for families that often cause nuisance to neighbours, drug-takers, alcoholics, people in and out of the prison system, or social care, children on the 'at risk' register, parents that are unable to parent well. Are these the people that George Osborne means when he talks about people watching TV with the curtains drawn while hard-working people trudge off to work?

> The families we work with are in very, very difficult circum-stances, emotionally, economically, socially they are very isolated. But I see them at one end of a continuum, because families in Britain are very stressed. Even if you take a family like mine, if you arrive on some days it would look totally crazy – but money papers over the cracks, and that is just not possible for some families, which makes crises impossible to deal with and means that the stresses and strains more quickly bring people to breaking point.

The approach of Participle has been based on a return to an old-fashioned, generic, multi-disciplinary support, based on listening to and working alongside families. The Life project works by inviting families to participate. They are at crisis point, or close to it, but it offers a lifeline before the authorities move in to evict them from their homes, or take their kids into care. The multi-disciplinary team is trained to work in a different way from the mainstream; they are expected to bring their own emotions and intuition into play; to empathise; to imagine. The staff have a range of professional disciplines but work together, sharing thinking and supporting each other. There is less form-filling, but more professional supervision. The workers that support each family are chosen, not by the managers, but by the families, who look for evidence of values, caring and commitment. The staff are not afraid of feeling or showing friendship for their clients. They bring care and kindness, as well as professional support. Such an approach is not 'soft' – indeed a truly engaged professional can be far more challenging, helping people to move out of a comfortable dependence into a more responsible freedom. But the response is judged by someone with 'unconditional positive regard' for the people they are caring for, who is not merely treating people as a unit.

I know, because I went to visit the project and met some of the families, that at least for some, this has worked. The engagement is voluntary – but commitment and effort is demanded. Project workers engage family members in conversation, rather than carry out assessments, and learn, quietly, while helping around the home, or minding the kids, about how they got into this fix, and what their hopes and aspirations are for getting out of it. In Swindon, Life project workers told me that 'most people want something better for their kids – only they don't always know how to get it'.

I listened to the story of one single mum whose two sons had been running wild and creating mayhem in their neighbourhood. At one stage she had marched them both to the council officers. 'You take them', she'd yelled, dumping them both in the social work offices. 'I give up.' Two workers from the project had worked with the family. One played pool with the boys, while the other went shopping with the mum. Slow, patient listening support had disentangled the anxiety of the young boys, who were testing for boundaries that never came, looking for love that was never expressed. The more their exploits led to anger and rejection, the more extreme they became. Their mum learned to contain her own anger, and to communicate the love she felt, but had never seen expressed in her own upbringing. Through a long painstaking relationship with the Life team, she had been able to reflect on her own needs, and learn to offer both love and boundaries; and the kids, finally getting what they needed, had calmed down and were now back at school. The family is getting closer, and things are getting better. A second family collapsed because the one sensible sister, who provided income and stability to her brothers, was made redundant. By supporting the strong member of the family, instead of simply trying to intervene in the lives of the damaged ones, the project could help them hold together. I heard from a man whose family had been about to lose their home through rent arrears about the struggle they had made to change things around, getting their kid back from care, beginning to volunteer in a local project, finally getting a job. None of this is easy. It's painstaking work. But as Hilary says:

> What we've got now is so expensive and so dramatically failing … so is there any reason for not changing?

At the time of our conversation, the onslaught against 'feckless families' had begun, so I pressed Hilary about this. Should there be limits to our social generosity? We talked earlier about people contributing and about assets. Should not everyone be expected to contribute?

> Of course there is something in there that chimes with me, because I believe that everyone should contribute, but what I also think is that those who don't contribute are so small in number – apparently social security fraud is only 0.7 per cent of the total – so it's completely absurd to build a whole way of looking at the world because of this tiny number of people.

She tells a story to illustrate about starting work on unemployment:

> We went to a job centre and we build a fake door, and said to the people in the jobs centre, 'if you want to get out of her and find work, come through this door!'. We asked people to pay a fiver

to come through the door, and eventually we raised it to £20, but still people wanted to come through our door, to get out of there and make something of themselves. Everyone in that job centre said 'get me out of here, give me a chance, get me away from these people who are doing nothing to contribute – get me to somewhere else where people are contributing and I can work with them and build a new life'. They all believed that they were the only genuine person wanting to make something of them-selves, and everyone else there were feckless losers. So that's a powerful narrative that people had internalised about 'people just like them'. It's very hard to build social solidarity and a different way of being and connectedness when you've got this meta-narrative about losers and feckless people.

Hilary argues persuasively against the underlying thinking that attempts to sort 'deserving from the undeserving'. She tells me that she has never met a family where at least one member doesn't want to get out of their difficulties and aspire to a better life. Rather than writing families off, she says, we should recognise and work with what it takes to help people turn their lives around. It would cost less than the hundreds of thousands we spend in trying to punish, teach and control.

Her view is that it's too hard to expect people to change on their own. They are up against a whole tide – diet, smoking, drinking, unemployment and mental health problems – and we can't just leave them to cope alone. When I persist in trying to identify those families that might be beyond the pale – fraudsters, criminals, the 'free-riders' – she challenges back:

I'm not worried, because I think there are relatively few of these people. So why don't we tell each other different stories and build up a better scenario and people will join in. The family work we do has taught me this. Even in the most desperate of circumstances, people want to build their capabilities. We need to challenge this over-dominance of economics. The frame we look at everything is through that economic language – 'free-rider' is an economic idea. As a social scientist interested in anthropology and psycho-analytic theory, what strikes me is how utterly painful and damaging and awful these people's lives are. You might say they are free riders, but does anyone really want to be that kind of person? Their lives are truly poor, by which I mean not economically poor, but limited. Where we have created a relationship that can be trusted, those families that have had the courage to work with us have been able to build a way out.

'KNOWING THE COST OF EVERYTHING AND THE VALUE OF NOTHING'

In the early decades of the welfare state, public sector workers were respected as professionals with a vocation, or seen as expert scientists and engineers bringing the latest knowledge to create a modern state. Professionals were assumed to be highly educated and trained, with a vocation for their work, and expected to apply their theoretical knowledge to exercise professional judgements; while the railways, the water companies, the power companies and other state enterprises were run as effective bureaucracies serving the public interest, and directly accountable to ministers.

At the end of the 1970s, however, the Thatcher government took power in the aftermath of the winter of discontent, arguing that public services had become poor value, and poor quality, hijacked by inefficient and lazy workers who had made their working lives comfortable at the expense of service users. There was just enough silliness and visible failure in public services to make this narrative convincing; and creaking, tatty public services were contrasted with a sleek, efficient, self-confident private sector (the myth that the private sector is more efficient has never really been challenged although the evidence has been far from convincing). Public services were sold off, cut back, or subject to 'compulsory competitive tendering'; they were treated as second best. Government wanted to measure and direct, to open the state to free competition, to find more efficient ways of doing things. Performance management systems were imported from the private sector: good service was no longer the responsibility of individual professionals – the doctors, the teachers the university professors – but in the hands of managers with the tools of 'business excellence', continuous improvement, motivational psychology, targets and change management programmes.

Between 1997 and 2010, while the Labour governments substantially increased public spending, they argued that if the public was to support this increase, services had to become efficient and far more effective – not only cutting costs but succeeding in achieving social outcomes. The Blair and Brown governments wanted to demonstrate not simply that public services were good value for money, but that they could achieve the social outcomes that society required: improving educational standards, reducing child poverty, increasing opportunities, reducing ill-health. To demonstrate those things required the measurement not simply of inputs and outputs, but compliance with good practice, and the evaluation of outcomes. And to feel safe, ministers wanted to drive this themselves, through a complex process of regulation and control – choosing evidence-based interventions at the centre and ensuring that the entire system could demonstrate that these interventions were being applied as intended, measuring and monitoring the work of each member of staff, each school, each university, each hospital.

The story is a complicated one, since some of the changes have been welcomed by both service users and staff as changing things for the better. Services now are more professional, more consistent, more focused, more efficient. Performance measurement and management has become part of our everyday assumptions of good practice. Across the public sector it's accepted that it's good to know what things cost, to try to achieve value for money, and to make processes efficient. We agree that we should evaluate whether what we do works, and whether it could work better. We need to be able to benchmark ourselves against others to see what we can learn and how we can improve. But the process of counting, measuring and controlling has a growing number of unintended consequences and perverse incentives. The measurements and targets are often clumsy proxies for what is really intended, and complex services, such as education, or health services, are trying to achieve many different things simultaneously. Professor Higgs, originator of the 'Higgs Bosun' commented in an interview about his retirement that he wouldn't be employed by a university today because they only measure performance through how many papers academics publish.

The process of increasing managerial control continues the trend of distrusting the competence of professionals. Ministers begin to try and take control of values and judgements, and instead of improving training, or conversation, or understanding, they tighten paperwork and process compliance. They no longer expected professionals to exercise their personal judgement: they are to be inspected, watched, advised, offered guidance, and ultimately expected to comply with performance regimes set at the centre. Processes are controlled through paperwork, and computers systems record every action, decision and choice for future audit and inspection. Every time something goes wrong, in a school, in a child safeguarding case, in a hospital, the media demand that the minister ensures 'it can never happen again', and the system becomes more risk-averse, the process of control tightens. All this means that professionals instead of working with patients and clients and students, spent more and more time in front of computers filling in forms and recording actions. Participle, in their work with troubled families, estimated that conventional social workers spent over eighty per cent of their time on paperwork, imputing data into computers and meetings with other professionals, and only twenty per cent of their time working with the families themselves. Worse, even the time spent in face to face contact with the families was often spent filling in forms and gathering data to 'feed the system'. It is of course possible to overstate the dangers here, because some of these system changes have undoubtedly improved safety and improved practice. But the scale of the shift towards compliance has been at huge financial and personal cost. This approach to efficiency – driven by major consultancies and learnt in the private sector – has had unforeseen consequences on the nature of our interactions with the state.

Public sector workers are subject to the same 'time and motion' men that for the last hundred years have dominated capitalist mass production: reducing pay, reducing terms and conditions, speeding up the production line. However, when you speed up a production line in the private sector you may exhaust the workers but the widgets are unaffected. But when the 'production line' is people, the impact of a speeded up work process may be elderly patients unable to reach water, or disabled people lifted too roughly. For some, but not all, public services – in care, education, health – the provider and the consumer are not simply engaged in a transaction. What matters most is the relationship, the care they take of each other, the amount they listen to each other, the sense of shared endeavour.

Somehow, in the process of creating these time-consuming and expensive compliance systems we have stripped professionals of the ability to exercise their skill, knowledge and judgement in their jobs, reducing both their satisfaction in their work, and their scope for exercising our full humanity in these roles. It's easy to assume that since we don't want poor or dangerous performance in our public services there is no alternative. But, as Hilary Cottam points out, all this risk aversion and control doesn't prevent harm. Insiders such as Eileen Monro, in her magisterial report into child protection, talks about the infantilisation of social workers, and about the need to improve working conditions, training, supervision, conversation and understanding. She says we have created 'a defensive system that puts so much emphasis on procedures and recording that insufficient attention is given to developing and supporting the expertise to work effectively with children, young people and families'.[1]

WHAT IS THE IMPACT OF PRIVATISATION?

It is perhaps too early to tell what the impact of privatisation is having on the values and the nature of the state. But it is a good question to ask. As more and more of the state's interactions with citizens are privatised and outsourced, private sector companies increasingly shape our experience of public services. What happens to our relationship to government in the process? Private companies no longer simply provide services, they are taking over

care and support, and regulatory and control functions also –
responsible for not only for hospitals and schools but for prisons
and probation, and access to benefits. Education and health care
become 'product lines' – the care industry is big business. Do
private sector values begin to undermine our expectations of the
state? We are only just beginning to see how the requirements for
competition and corporate business growth impact on the relationships between the citizen and the state. They may, in some
areas, be a breath of fresh air, offering more choice-based, and
more user-based solutions, challenging long-established practice,
paying more attention to customers. But the relationship is never
a simple one. Private-sector companies can introduce the
semblance of a provider-consumer relationship, but that is never
the whole story – accountability to government caps the money
that can be spent, and limits and constrains the solutions that can
be found. Choice is often an illusion when resources are rationed.
Benefits claimants have no more choice when their claims are
processed by a private company: the contract is with the government, and the complaints procedures and appeals process have
been determined by the client. The very nature of large-scale
contracting can make it harder for front-line staff to respond flexibly to citizens – they have scripts to recite and procedures to
follow, to make sure that the service is standardised. Systems like
payment by results are intended to bring radical private sector
thinking and dynamism into tired government processes – and in
some cases this may work – but the financial requirements of
measuring, counting, replicating and standardising tend in the
opposite direction. As 'consumers' of a private sector service, our
sense of powerlessness can grow: people on benefits can't hold the
line indefinitely for computerised phone systems; older people
fail to make sense of on-line access systems; single phone numbers
go unanswered. Our interactions with privatised government can
feel like 'computer says no'. It is often hard to trace the basic
elements of democratic accountability through the layers of
contracting and sub-contracting, to private suppliers and corporate systems. Should organisations that provide public services
open their books? Should their governance processes be trans-

parent? Should they account to citizens at local level as well as to national government? How do we investigate and approve their actions on our behalf? We have only just begun to think about how we build robust relationships and accountability within the privatised state.

CAN THE STATE BE HUMAN?

If we see welfare as something to be eked out, to be denied where possible, if we try to 'keep people out' of services designed to help, if we spend more money separating out the undeserving from the deserving or hunting down fraud than we spend on the service itself, that says a lot about the sort of society we are becoming. David Marquand was concerned about the perverse incentives government can set up in its efforts to generate efficiency – speeding up care, not paying attention: 'if you set up a system to incentivise cruel things that's what they will do'. He talked about the need to develop relationships of trust, and about how we respond perversely if we are not trusted: 'If you develop a system with the tacit premise that you can't trust your staff, then your staff will become untrustworthy'. We discussed the terrible experiences of Mid-Staffordshire hospital, where patients were denied proper care, or the care home where adults with learning disabilities were tortured by their carers. Hilary Cottam argues that:

> being a cog in a machine makes you sick – figuratively and liter-
> ally – and people who are treated as a component in a computer
> cease to bring their full human cognitive powers to work. The
> only way to survive in a machine-based system as a worker is to
> shut down, so that you really don't see it.

We somehow make the state more stupid than it needs to be, because humans are capable of careful nuanced judgements, but the systems we create are 'dumbed down' to ensure compliance. If we want a society in which we are all treated as 'ends in themselves' and not means, in which the full humanity of everyone can be realised, we need to think hard about the state. Victor Adebowale talked about the need to go back to first principles. He challenges the assumption that the public sector is bloated or too bureaucratic, and argues that private sector companies can be equally flawed, equally bloated, equally bureaucratic. 'One sees no necessary improvement if we replace the public sector with the private sector, it doesn't make the service any more human'. 'But can the state provide human, kind services?' I asked.

> Of course it can. It's possible for bureaucracies to be kind, that's about the culture of the people inside it. It's about service to the public – services that treat people as individuals and not numbers, regardless of whether it's public or private. We should be able to expect the public sector to treat us with care, kindness and wisdom.

Victor argues that the trend towards performance management and targets is neither inevitable, nor certain:

> We are learning about the failing of this approach. We know that targets don't produce improved performance. They produce people who perform to the targets. We are more sophisticated than that. There is a tendency to take a short cut, turn everything into burger flipping. But the public don't respond well to burger flipping.

He argues that what matters most is a culture of learning, of exploration; one in which staff have the responsibility and the freedom to learn and to change in response to what they learn. Kind organisations have the time to think, to respond differently to different circumstances; staff are able to explore and learn, and have the freedom to make good judgements: 'Cultures are created, they are not accidents, and the culture we create – in the public, private or voluntary sector – could be one in which we treat people differently'.

Leo Boland has explored ways of thinking about the difference between the 'system' and the 'lifeworld' using the work of Habermas.[2] For Habermas, the 'system' encompasses both private corporate and government organisations: rule-governed, bureaucratic, treating people as units rather than as individuals. To Habermas, writing in the aftermath of Nazi Germany and Stalinist Russia, there is an ever-present danger of 'the system', whether capitalism or the state, dehumanising us. In opposition to the system he describes the 'life-world', the world of relationships, family bonds of friendship, kinship, idiosyncratic relationships and empathy. In the life-world we are not treated identically, we are encountered as individuals with unique characteristics and needs. The life-world is not necessarily benign (it is in the life-world that husbands beat wives and wives murder husbands), but it is a world in which emotions, needs and our unique humanity are noticed. In the system, we are units. Most of us only encounter the state in its full controlling impact at moments of crisis – or occasions of great importance – adopting a child, recording a death, having a baby, trying to get help for an aged parent. We are often shocked by the formality, the form-filling, the inflexibility. But for some families, those with damaged lives and chaotic lifestyles, with addictions or mental illness, with physical disability or learning difficulties, whole lives are spent under the system's eye – every move is monitored, every shift in income reported, every change of circumstance reassessed. It is to these people, the most damaged, the most dependent, that the value system and attitudes of bureaucrats and professionals makes the difference between deepening misery or offering enlightened help.

There is a libertarian tradition on both left and right that argues that because of the state's inevitable rule-governed bureaucratic approach, it is safer to keep the state small, and to leave our private lives private. But this is to leave us as individuals entirely vulnerable to the 'openness' of markets, and powerless to protect ourselves against far more powerful institutions. Habermas would argue that the tentacles of the corporate sector are just as powerful, conditioning and controlling our choices in ways that shape our lives far more than governments do. An alternative approach would be to welcome the role of government in holding back corporate power and creating spaces that are not dominated by cash transactions – but to find ways of humanising the way it works.

Janet Daby, a former social worker manager who is now a councillor, who we will meet more fully in the next chapter, said that public sector organisations meant well but somehow were not as effective or creative as they could be and often missed the point:

> You get driven to a standstill because of the bureaucracy, the paperwork, it's so all-consuming that you can't do the real job you came to do. Somehow we have created care organisations that don't feel as if they care. They are supposed to provide a caring service but they can often feel as if they are authoritarian, controlling. Police officers, social workers, nurses sometimes lose that sense of sensitivity and empathy. I've been in hospital where you feel like you've lost your identity – you've become a nobody. The staff need support to be permitted to show their caring side.

CAN THE STATE LOVE?

Thinking a bit further about the implications of all this, and reflecting on Hilary Cottam's experience earlier in this chapter, raises a number of further issues. If love is one of the healing relationships we human beings have with each other, what happens when people rely for care on the state? Can government institutions provide the affection, the trust, the reciprocity, that people need to thrive? Can the state love?

Of course, we need the state to uphold civic and democratic values, to be free from corruption, to treat citizens equally, to be fair, and prudent. These values remain. Across the public sector, equality, safeguarding and human rights are now taken more seriously, and that is good, and right, but there are other values that we need to sustain. The attitudes and behaviours of workers, front line staff, receptionists, professionals, managers – create our 'experience' of the state. That experience does not have to be one of coldness, or inflexibility. We can change it.

If the state were to create the conditions for an open tribe, we would start with values that underpin openness – listening, enquiry, curiosity. We would expect staff in any state service to show respect to everyone, however frail, however newly arrived.

We would want them to be curious, taking an interest in the unique experience of everyone they encounter, willing to take the time to hear their story and to understand their circumstances. We would look for empathy, an ability to put themselves in the shoes of every patient, asylum-seeker or student. We would want imagination and creativity, a willingness to explore situations fully in order to discover new solutions. We would want them to show care and kindness, so that even when administering highly rule-governed procedures, they would never be cruel or offensive.

We would want to see courage in the face of bureaucratic obstacles, and in the pursuance of duty – courage to whistle-blow or to challenge organisational heartlessness, but also the courage of a social worker to knock on the door of a house where abuse is suspected, or where trafficked girls might be trapped: the courage of a teacher to discuss female genital mutilation; or the courage of a psychiatric nurse to pursue an intuition about a potential suicide. We would not want our public servants to hide behind procedural rules and to cover up laziness. We would want them to be explorers, seeking for public good and for the well-being of the people they serve. Finally, and most important, we would want wisdom, the ability to make careful, balancing judgements, because the things we want and need are often contradictory and it takes a lively human intelligence to make sense of this and make sensible decisions about competing needs. We want public servants to bring their whole human intelligence and sensitivity to bear on the problems that face our society.

Hilary Cottam talked about the positive experience people had working with Participle, precisely because it was a different approach to work: 'lots of people want to join us. Social workers don't want to just fill in forms, they want to use their skills to help people change their lives for the better'. But she warns that the past few decades have deskilled professionals, so that they no longer have the experience to make complex judgements, nor the skills to support people in complex changes to their ways of thinking and acting. She points out that if we were to return to greater professional autonomy and a stress on relationships, we would have to recruit different people, with different skills. The kinds of changes she is advocating have implications also for management, and for the way people learn their profession, and for the work process itself:

> To bring the whole person to work is very exhausting, so we need lower case-loads and really good, professionally trained supervision, not just management supervision. Supervision needs to be nurturing, stretching, and we need to create space for teams to reflect together, because this is really difficult work. The culture of the team is also highly relational. You can't expect people to deliver relationship services with a back office and management system of a bureaucracy.

When I asked what we would have to do to create this approach more widely, she worried that we didn't have the skills any more to work like this. We would need to rediscover them:

> Change and development for anyone is an emotional engagement, a conversation, a relationship. It is very different from the way we've structured our services these days. The more I do this work, the more I become alarmed that in our public services the developmental context has been hollowed out.

THE STATE AS A RELATIONSHIP

If we want to change the nature of work, a good place to start would be in public services. We discussed in the past chapter ways to make work more meaningful, more democratic and more creative. We could start with the work of millions of people whose work is supposed to improve society, but who currently feel disempowered, exhausted, dispirited. Only empowered people can empower others. If we want to ensure that people who work in education, care, housing, employment, skills and benefits, bring their whole human selves to work, we need to shift from a compliance culture to a culture of enquiry.

The implications are profound – but none of this is new. In the 1970s, Donald Schon wrote about the 'reflective practitioner' in social work, using every encounter with a service user to learn and change – co-creating solutions with clients – never doing the same thing twice.[3] If we were to seriously set out across our public services to restore empathy, creativity, judgement and balance, we would need to allow professionals to experiment, to restore to all training a sense of open discussion and exploration. Instead of policy and standards being set at the centre, we would expect each group of professionals to discuss, to challenge, to support each other in thinking about their own boundaries and priorities, asking questions such as 'who's side are we on?', 'what are the limits to our capability?', 'what can and can't we tackle?' – rather than relying on procedure manuals and 'following orders'. The centre, management, Whitehall, can never anticipate every eventuality, can never foresee the millions of human encounters, and should not try to control them. That doesn't, of course, mean that there are no rules and no boundaries, but that professionals in conversation with their service users constantly remake those rules in response to their experiences.

If we want the state to be human, we have to acknowledge as citizens that we need to react as humans too. It's not just state workers who need to bring their whole selves to encounters and relationships. As citizens, we can do more, in our interactions with the state, and with each other, than react as passive customers. If we want the state, and society, to treat us well, we need to recipro-cate. Each encounter should be ruled by good manners, on both sides. We should treat others as we would wish to be treated. In the life-world, underlying the most basic human kindness are some unspoken rules – protect the weak from the strong, put the comfort of others before your own. Common courtesy and decency get us a long way.

An encounter should always be seen as reciprocal – as involving two people giving and receiving – even if it is only thanks. We should recognise the effort another has made, and give respect. We should ensure that others can conduct themselves with dignity at all times, and not demean or patronise another person. We should recognise the reality of political choices that lead to rationing, rather than blaming public sector workers, or demonising people who are not, under the current rules, entitled.

We need to accept that this is a relationship, and not a cash transaction, and that other people's needs might be greater than our own. A GP once said to me 'if we stop being willing to wait, and queue, the NHS is finished!' Queuing is a gesture of courtesy, a recognition of our relationships to others. It isn't muscling forward but holding back, respecting the fact that others were here first. The problem of bringing private sector assumptions into public service is that we want, all of a sudden, to demand, to push, to feel an entitlement. But being human is to put others before ourselves, the weak before the strong. My old family GP, before any appointment systems were created, used to simply see everyone who turned up to the surgery. But he didn't operate a first-come first-serve policy, he chose to see the frail, the burdened, the pregnant, those with young children first, and the able-bodied, middle-class, busy professionals last. He made judgements about whose needs were greatest. We respected that. He would also call in, unexpectedly, to see if you were recovered after an illness. No-one does that any more.

The attempt to turn public services into a market place and citizens into consumers encourages greed, unrealistic expectations, bad manners and selfishness. We may not be able to have everything we want, but we should trust that our society will help us to have what we need.

NOTES

1. Eileen Munro, *The Munro Review of Child Protection: A Child-Centred System*, Department of Education, London 2011.
2. For this argument, see Leo Boland, 'Can the Leviathan stop eating people', in Sue Goss and Katherine Kerswell (eds), *Challenging Behaviour*, Solace 2009 – which also acknowledges the work of Frank Fruchtel in this field.
3. Donald A. Schon, *The Reflective Practitioner: How Professionals Think in Action*, Basic Books 1983.

6. CHANGE ALWAYS STARTS
AT THE EDGE

It's not as if the ideas we have been discussing are new or untested. In many places experiments are already underway. Change has already started. The future, as the saying goes, is already here. It's just unevenly distributed. Howard Jarche, a change guru, has written about 'moving to the edges', where there is more challenge and more creativity 'where the answers may not be clear, but they are less obscured than in the centre'.[1] David Marquand believes that if we want to find evidence of change, the last place to look would be Westminster. Instead, he suggests looking at Scotland, Wales, Northern Ireland, and at English local government and the regions.

Perhaps the most important example in the UK of a different sort of politics has been the Good Friday Agreement: a process in which politicians from opposing sides, with decades of violent conflict and hatred behind them, slowly, painfully, negotiated a settlement. Radically, this was an 'agreement to disagree', an acknowledgement that there were two different views of the future and both were legitimate. It was an agreement between people who did not share the same goals, but could agree about a way of living with the differences – and, crucially, could co-create the institutions and social processes to allow co-existence. All parties to the agreement signed up to 'partnership, equality and mutual respect as the basis of relationships'.[2] This was an extraordinary process of listening, compromising, back-sliding, changing, with a recognition on all sides that the first agreement would not 'solve' the centuries-old tensions in the north – but it might begin a journey. So strongly understood was this notion of a journey with stops and starts and set-backs that even now, when violence flares up, it is possible for some sensible politicians and citizens on all sides to talk about how long change takes, and not automatically talk of betrayal or 'giving in'.

But the process didn't start with the politicians. It started somewhere else. Two women from across the catholic and protestant communities joined hands. Mairead Corrigan responded to the death of her sister's children in a tragic accident with a getaway car, by demonstrating for peace, and was joined by Betty Williams, who saw the incident; and between them they brought thirty thousand catholic and protestant women together, culminating in a march of thirty-five thousand people. At first they were called Women for Peace, but this gave way to calling themselves simply 'The Peace People'. Purna Sen describes the inspiration this gave:

> During the time of the peace process you had two groups of women, one from the protestant community and one from the catholic community, carrying out this sort of experiment. They talked about putting themselves in the other person's shoes. They were not saying it didn't matter that they were protestant and catholic, but that what they had in common was being women and from marginalised communities, and they shared an experience of feeling excluded from a politics that was very male. So they wanted to break that down.

The Scottish constitutional convention in the run-up to devolution was another experiment in a different kind of democracy. Parties, social institutions, the churches and business federations came together to begin a process of debate about what a devolved Scotland might be like, laying the foundations for the transition to devolved government in 1998. Unusually, political parties worked together within this alliance – the Labour Party, Liberal Party and Scottish Greens (but not the Nationalists, who felt the process was too Labour dominated). What was unique about the Constitutional Convention was that it was a process of consensus building, of exploration, of imagination; it was not simply a re-run of the same old adversarial battles. Scotland would be a different place now, had it not been for that process.

Interestingly, in 2014 the Scottish referendum debate does not seem to involve the same bringing together of formal politics with civil society: there seems to be a 'politicians' debate' between the political parties, but outside of that a different, wider conversation about what the future might be like. In my conversation with Willie Sullivan, we discuss his experience of what is going on in Scotland:

> The referendum debate itself is quite dry, conducted through the normal political process, and is all about the currency and the euro. But beneath that there are some far more interesting things going on, because, of course, the bigger question that it makes us all face is, 'what sort of country do we want to be?' Scots are beginning to look northwards to Scandinavia and want to explore how they do things, since you could say that Scotland is almost a Nordic country, and they do things differently there. Suddenly there are lots of people coming over from Nordic countries and lots of people going the other way to investigate.

Some of the ideas being explored are about what it would mean to be a more equal society:

> We hear that the UK is the second most unequal country in the OECD, and Nationalists and those who think that Scotland should be independent are beginning to say 'why would we want to be such an unequal country?'. We are the fourth wealthiest country in the world but our resources are unequally distributed. We know from the *Spirit Level* and other research that inequality has a huge impact on everything – from teenage pregnancy to mental health. Unequal states do worse, while in Scandinavia and other parts of northern Europe, where there's less inequality, people seem to do better. What we are learning from the Nordic states is that fiscal policy on its own does not address inequality. In fact if you look at the Nordic states the UK has a more progressive tax policy than they do. But we've started to realise that inequality is not solved by mildly redistributive taxation. In the UK there is such a vast inequality in what people get paid; and

our low-pay, low-skill economy creates inequality. People are just not getting paid enough. The difference between us and Sweden is about the way that the economy and society are structured. So, for example, Sweden has since the 1970s seen free childcare as a way of creating equality.

And while it is probably true, as Willie explains, that the traditions of Scotland are more collectivist, and social democracy there is a strong tradition, what's interesting is not just the subjects of political debate, but the way politics is conducted:

A lot of people are interested in learning. So some Scottish women who were in Iceland during the crowd-sourcing of the constitution and the constitutional convention came back and started talking to other people about it, and then people from Iceland came to Scotland. There's a think tank been set up by Lesley Riddick called Nordic Horizons, which has been organising exchanges and bringing people to speak in Edinburgh at events that are completely sold out every time. These things are not being led by the conventional political parties. The national parties are playing catch-up most of the time. Many of the ideas are coming from Common Weal, a group of thinkers, academics and activists; and then you have another interesting group, the Radical Independence Campaign, a broad left movement who see independence as a means to a radical left agenda, who can get a thousand people in a room – which is big for Scotland.

I ask if there is not a danger that this is just a very small group of people talking to themselves. Was this simply a gathering of the chattering classes of Scotland?

I think the test is whether these ideas and this analysis gain any popular support. I don't think the only way for this energy to be captured is to win a yes vote. The ideas, the enthusiasm and the engagement with the question of what a better country could be like – that's not going to go away. After the referendum, of course, there is the potential for this to be stamped down, and over a period of time for people to become disappointed and disillusioned. But there is also an opportunity for the energy to be carried forward, to keep going.

Listening to Willie, I thought perhaps the challenge for the rest of the UK is whether we could create the same energy around the same questions, without the catalyst of an independence referendum.

In Wales, of course, as I discovered in my conversation with Lee Waters, Director of the Institute of Welsh Affairs and a leading journalist and commentator, things are different. As Lee says:

Wales and Scotland are often seen as alike, but we're not very alike at all. Scotland has been an independent country far more recently, and had its own legal system and institutions which it has kept. So it always had more solid foundations for a different civil society. Wales has only had devolved government for fifteen years – so we are creating a new democratic society. We've come a very long way in those fifteen years, but there is still a long way to go. Usually, when new democracies are created, there is a process led by civil society rising up, and democratic change happens as a result of major social movements, but in Wales we have a new settlement that was created by the political elite. So we don't have a civil society holding the government's feet to the fire as often happens after a radical governmental change. We've always had politics in Wales, but what is new is Welsh politics. We are at the beginning of creating a new democratic culture.

The initial referendum was very close, but now there is growing support for more power, and very soon the parliament will have taxation powers: 'firing with live ammunition' as Lee puts it.

Lee talks about the collaborative benefits of being a very small country – the population is only three million people – and gives an example:

Everyone knows each other, so the upside is that it is much easier to establish coalitions and alliances when there is a consensus. Two years ago there was a cross-party consensus on electrifying the mainline railway. Westminster just wanted to electrify as far as Cardiff, but a coalition was created to extend the electrification to Swansea and the valleys' lines. It was a cross-party movement, led by business and civil society, and because it was so sensible there was strong agreement across the Assembly, which meant that Liberal Democrats could talk to their coalition ministers about it. All the parties went together in a delegation to London. Afterwards I met a group of Welsh Labour MPs and they were amazed; they said there was no way that could have happened about an English issue; there they were far too locked into tribal politics to work together.

But the flipside of this, he says, can be a cosiness, a lack of challenge and a self-censorship which means that radical thinking doesn't happen. Labour is no longer working with Plaid Cymru in government, and the collapse of the rainbow-coalition idea of a Liberal-Democrat, Plaid Cymru and Conservative opposition means that Labour looks unassailable in Wales, reducing the pressure for change. 'You need the support of the Welsh government to achieve most things now in Wales, so you tend not to want to make enemies.' He talks about the problems of having a weak civil society, a weak media, and social institutions that are not yet used to working at a Welsh level – for many civil society organisations the Welsh organisation is seen as peripheral. Without a strong civil society, policy-making is poor: there are not the experts, the NGOs, the think tanks, the opinion formers and the research establishments to offer ideas or challenge government thinking:

> There is an emerging generation who sees things differently and think differently, but they're not the generation who are in power. It will take time. They're starting to emerge into positions of leadership – people my age and younger – and their assumptions are different. Civil society is playing catch up but we will get there.

As an example he talks about the potential for crowd-sourcing new Welsh policy:

The Institute of Welsh Affairs has set up a pilot project to look at the devolution of policing to Wales. We brought fifty people together online – police officers, judges, academics, etc – to have a conversation within a safe space. It was a difficult topic to pick, but we saw the potential of this approach to involve people.

Now they are looking at ways to get funding for further crowd-sourcing around the future of the NHS in Wales:

There is a really important role for such a project because changes have to be made: the financial problems are growing, but it is really difficult for the political establishment to face up to them. There's a lack of richness in the current policy debate, and if we can create a safe space where people can come together we start to bring out new ideas, create a richness of debate, a space where ideas collide: where people can try things out and begin to build alternatives, producing the energy we have been missing, a plat-form for us to build new answers.

OTHER EXPERIMENTS

Across Europe there are all sorts of experiments to learn from. Iceland's radical post-crash government brought together nearly a thousand randomly selected citizens to brainstorm a process for creating a new constitution. Their ideas led to the election of twenty-five Assembly members from 522 ordinary candidates (including lawyers, political scientists, journalists, professors as well as politi-cians), who in turn opened up their process to the public through Wikipedia, Twitter, Facebook, YouTube and Flickr. They discussed proposals on fifty radio show presentations, and the constitutional council streamed their proceedings to Twitter and Facebook, with uploads on Flickr and videos on Youtube. The referendum vote on the new constitution involved just over a third of the Icelandic population, of whom a substantial majority were in favour, but the process has now stalled after legal challenges followed by the election in 2013 of a government opposed to the new constitution's ratifica-tion. However, as an experiment it has been remarkable.

In Denmark, Alternativet (The Alternative) is creating a stir as a radical 'open source' party. Anyone is welcome to suggest polices and help build the manifesto and the aim is to create 'popular political laboratories, both on a digital platform but also face to face, in physical meetings', with ideas that will be voted on at the party's first meeting in June 2014.[3] The idea is to reach out 'to political individuals and groups that are deeply involved in network-based politics but until now have been rightly disinterested in traditional "top-down party politics"'.[4]

LOCAL GOVERNMENT

In English local government, too, experiments are underway that challenge assumptions about politics and politicians. Greater Manchester brings together a coalition of councils to tackle regional problems; Cornwall experimented with creating an open source technology platform to enable local communities to put forward solutions to local problems; Wigan is harnessing untapped community resources to support social care through volunteering and developing micro-enterprises;[5] Devon is in conversation with activist towns like Totnes to devolve responsibility for many services; Cheshire West and Chester has created a series of public service mutuals, to run council services. City regions are becoming ambitious for their local economies, but also determined to tackle deprivation and poverty, for example through improving life chances for the under-fives or reducing obesity. In some areas the NHS and local councils are beginning to work together. In Hackney the local authority and health services are working with community groups to build a shared campaign to stamp out FGM. Elsewhere, schools are being turned into 'neighbourhood hubs' from which health and other services can reach more people; charities and civil society groups are taking over libraries and bringing in new ideas. Despite – or more probably because of – taking the brunt of the Coalition government's austerity measures, local councils are finding innovative ways to enable services to survive. This innovation is not the preserve of any single political party. It is deep connections to a place, passion about a community and the determination to protect local people that is driving the change. These changes don't always find favour with the trades unions and the traditional left: cuts are being made, and the involvement of social enterprises and mutuals is seen by some as privatisation. But councils are also in the forefront of the living wage campaign, and the campaign against pay-day loan companies.

From the perspective of an open tribe, what is perhaps most promising is the role that local authorities have decided to play in creating community cohesion, and bringing different sections of society together. Oldham, for example, suffered from very troubled relationships between opposing, closed communities, and the Council deliberately set out to offer help in creating community cohesion and reducing community tension. The Council has begun to change the dynamics in the community by means of number of different initiatives: through plays, cultural activities and festivals; through training staff to reach and respond to all communities; through supporting the development of leadership in the voluntary sector and communities; through supporting networks of community activists; through creating public spaces where people can come together and explore differences and build shared ways forward; through developing 'community agreements' in key neighbourhoods; through explicitly supporting the development of women into leadership; through responding to hate crime. A conference held in 2007 invited the different communities to come together, to 'have your say, hear from others, meet new people, share your success and have fun along the way'. It directly asked questions such as: 'should people from different communities mix more?', 'does it matter?', 'why do "they" want to be friends with "us"?', 'how can we make life better for those who have the least?'.

Under its young leader Jim McMahon, the Council has begun to experiment in how it connects to its residents – full council meetings are web-streamed online, watched by 300 people; and people can ask live questions and join the debate via Facebook, Twitter and email. The Oldham Youth Council has constitutional power, and a section on the council agenda to raise issues. An open council session allows ward members to ask questions, and each councillor issues an annual report about how they have spent their time and their budget, while councillors have to attend a compulsory leadership course to learn leadership behaviours. Jim McMahon talks in his blog about the fact that when Oldham faced real financial and managerial difficulties there was 'no time for adversarial politics'; leaders from across all the main parties worked together to find solutions. Even now that the Council has a firm Labour majority, the leader still works with the opposition leaders to chew over the big issues facing their local economy and city. Named as the 'sixth unhappiest place to be in England' by Rightmove, there was a lot to get right. The Council now pays the living wage, has set up an hours-bank to save the tax credits of part-timers, and is tackling pay-day loans and unscrupulous rent-to-buy retailers.[6]

The London Borough of Lambeth, too, has tried to create an experimental 'collaborative council'. The model is about 'giving people more involvement and control of the services they use and the places they live by putting council resources in their hands':

Cooperation between service providers, such as the council, and those who use or are affected by services, such as residents and communities, has resulted in public services that are more aligned with people's needs and expectations.[7]

Their philosophy is about enabling, and encouraging citizens to share responsibility for services and to take control over libraries, play-schemes, etc. Some of these experiments have outraged traditional trades-unionists and the left.[8] They are taking place against a backdrop of 30 per cent cuts or more in council spending, and the Council has been accused of asking communities to cut their own services. But the councillors argue that when money is very scarce it is even more important to share power and bring community resources to bear to protect badly needed services and facilities. Lambeth has set up time-banks to enable people to be rewarded for volunteering, and has established volunteering projects in parks and green spaces. The arts team act as facilitators, connecting citizens and communities together, making things happen. This is a more holistic approach: the local authority is not seen as the 'decider and provider' but as creating the democratic framework within which collective decisions are made and collaborative actions planned.

Jack Hopkins, the councillor in Lambeth responsible for safer and stronger neighbourhoods, has been experimenting with projects that put the community in charge of decisions:

> The public were fed up of being consulted loads of different times about different proposals, so we wanted to take a neighbourhood approach and put all the budget together for one overall consultation. We decided to let the community design the consultation for themselves, so we sent out postcards asking: 'how can we make your walk to school easier', 'how can we make your street better', and then sat down with community groups to work out exactly what the problems were; we let them decide how to solve the problem. So they worked up the schemes they wanted – which might be traffic calming or environmental schemes – and then we brought the residents' groups together to discuss them, because often their groups only covered a street or a few streets, and we wanted them to see how all the schemes would affect them, and influence all of them. After all a cycle route can go through lots of neighbourhoods. I used ideas I'd borrowed from a politician in Chicago, about participatory budgeting, but also including a public ballot so that residents could decide between the schemes. That meant that if a community group wanted a scheme they had to persuade others to vote for it. And since the budget was limited, that meant agreeing priorities with each other. The council acted as facilitators and neutral arbiters – with ward councillors able to make decisions. In one area it was very controversial, and the community held four or five meetings to reach a decision, but they worked it out in the end. In another case, a community group proposed a really expensive scheme, with York stone and Victorian lampposts, but when they saw that they would be taking up most of the budget, instead of fighting for it against the other groups, they went away and reduced the cost of their scheme.

We learnt that the transport planners often proposed big expensive schemes, but local people tended to want little things – road humps or pocket parks or small green spaces. In one area we built up the road to pavement height so that the local café could have tables outside. I didn't want the transport planners to say 'that's not my job' – and so if people also had ideas about social issues we would take them on board. Some of the traffic planners left, because they didn't think this fitted with their 'professional' assessments of need, but others started to go out and talk to people, started talking to schools about what would make things safer. One persuaded GPs to pay for improvements outside the surgery. One of the transport planners said to me, 'this has reminded me of why I came into this work in the first place'.

The Council has launched a digi-buddy scheme, recognising that the most vulnerable people may get left behind in the digital revolution. The scheme trains volunteers to train people in the community to use computers – making sure that job seekers and the elderly are not left behind as transactions are increasingly shifted online. And they have harnessed support from Jobs Centre Plus, local churches and community centres, and are equipping 300 volunteers to train local people.

There's even an experiment in co-production around licensing, where communities sit down with pubs and clubs that are seen as creating noise or nuisance, to co-create a set of guidelines that will enable them to co-exist peaceably – with the sanction that the community will gather the evidence to enable action under licensing laws if negotiations fail.

A NEW SORT OF POLITICIAN?

There is a stereotypical image of a local councillor which still rings true in many places; councillors tend to be older than the population, and are more likely to be white and male. We imagine councillor sitting behind mahogany tables in committee rooms for long tedious meetings. But not all local politicians are like that.

For example, meet Janet Daby, a young councillor in the London borough of Lewisham. Her story began when she discovered that no-one much came to her surgery, though she knew that, since her ward was one of the most deprived in London, that couldn't be because her constituents had no problems:

> I'd hear stories from staff at the local community centre that some children were going to school hungry, and from the care-taker on the estate that parents were going hungry to feed their children. This concerned me. I wanted to help. I was reminded of my driving lesson, which taught me to anticipate potential dangers and hazards, and my social work training when I was taught to reduce the risk of harm to children. So, if my constit-uents were facing the pending benefit changes of bedroom tax and benefit cuts then I needed to anticipate my role in all of this. I was used to action planning through my work, so I wrote on a flipchart at home the needs in the area, key organisations and who I would like to work with in the community. I needed a team!
>
> Funding was also a consideration. So then I contacted local churches in the area – Church of England, Evangelical, Pentecostal and a free church. A community worker knew one of the vicars well and introduced us (he has since become a key partner in our project). Initially, I just explored what might be possible, and when some weren't keen I just asked them come along and if they wanted to pull out later, that would be fine. So they came to an informal meeting. I involved people I knew as well as new people, including a social enterprise called Eco-Communities which has taken over three of the libraries in Lewisham, a Pastor who had already run a food-bank and knew how to do it well, and finally my husband who is creative. The steering group was formed, with me as the main driver, pulling, pushing and holding it together.
>
> So, following much discussion and planning, we started with a food project, but I didn't want this to be just a voluntary project. I wanted the Council to be involved – not to take over, but to create a two-way exchange, sharing, learning and

working together in the area. I approached a nutritionist in Public Health and asked her to get involved, but she did not take me up on the offer. However her colleague did, and she now assists us with monitoring the service and with health links. The food project offers health advice, advice about baby nutrition, and cooking skills classes, and is linked to a charity called 'delicious nutritious', a voluntary group of mums who have learnt how to cook and are starting a business, and are now teaching volunteers how to teach others. Every Thursday evening, anything between 20 to 40 people come to the food project for food, and alongside it we have a partnership area where people can speak to someone about what else they need. I or my fellow local councillor are there if they need help from us, and we have debt advice from a voluntary CAB worker; Phoenix Community Gateway Housing conduct a housing surgery, and there is support with setting up your own business, CV writing, and benefits support. Also there to help are the Pre-School Learning Alliance, Carers Support and the Parents Support Group. The church also offers pastoral care should someone wish to speak to them. We now have four users of the project who have begun to volunteer.

She talks about Alex, a young drug addict who started by using the food project bank but now is one of her most energetic volunteers:

> He says that the only day of the week he doesn't smoke dope is the day he comes to the food project. He's got such a deep sense of purpose, he feels wanted and valuable, and it's a reason to have a clean day. So I am beginning to think what can we do for him on the other days. How can we help him spend them differently – as well as other drug addicts? What else needs to change locally and nationally to bring about such drastic and positive change?

Her enthusiasm for the project bubbles over. They've now been offered a whole building by one of the churches, and she tells me about plans for a discussion group for teenagers, and a film night, help for older people in using computers, support for start-up new businesses and coffee mornings for people who just want some company. What is impressive is not just the plans, but the way she goes about things. She's concerned to make sure that neither she nor the Council takes over the energy and ideas of local people. Her politics about showing what is possible and then listening: 'The danger is that you say all the right things but don't listen. It needs to be a two-way process. What if the Labour Party was to actually encourage people to develop their own policies?'

She also talks about bringing together a parenting group from troubled families to form their own ideas about what they need:

> You know, most people who have experienced hardship have some pretty good ideas about what would make a difference. And then, when they've formulated some ideas about what they need, they need the politicians to come to listen and to help them form their ideas into policy and practice. If you were to adopt the principles of sitting down and hearing each other out, you would bring in all the experience and knowledge that you have, but you also add all the experience and knowledge that others have. It's about building trust, because when you've got trust, you can say 'well, I don't think that's going to work', and they will hear you. What I want is for the Council not to need to be in control, but to listen, support, help to organise, see what works – but putting everyone on the same level so that it's not a hierarchy with the Council saying what you can and can't do. A lot of the parents are professional people with their own experience and skills. Local government can help and support by bringing people together instead of doing it for them or to them.

She pauses and then she says: 'You know the support that people really need? It's friendship, relationships, to know that someone cares and cares enough to do something.'

Jack Hopkins talks about the importance of space for people to come together:

> The people who are most active in community groups are generally well-heeled, and I have no problem about that. But it's

important that they meet the people from the estates across the road, and understand their lives, so that they understand what they need. It's our job to help people to understand each other and get along with each other.

We have a really active Portuguese community, and when we were having meetings about building a street market it was suggested that it should be a Portuguese-themed market, to attract visitors. But at the meetings local people were grumbling about 'the bloody Portuguese'. So I said 'what about Miguel, who's on the residents' committee – he makes a great contribution. And they were all, 'oh he's all right', and I was saying 'just listen to yourselves' … in a conversation you can do that. We learn by listening and understanding each other. It's the conversation that's important…

The differences that open up between people are all about not understanding each other – the gap between communities from different backgrounds is the same as the gap between older people and young people, middle-class and working-class. We've lost a lot of the places where people can go and mix together – there are fewer and fewer shared spaces. If people don't feel included or feel 'this isn't for me' they can feel awkward and defensive. We need to create spaces for people to meet and intermingle, places where there is no profit and loss account. A local library is important, not just because of the books, but because it's a free space where people can get out of the rain and read the paper. It's a space where we can run events and bring people together.

We have to realise how important space can be. If you're middle-class you have space. But if you live on an estate, and you share a bedroom and have a row with your parents or your partner, or you need somewhere to do your homework, where do you go? The only place kids can go is to hang out around street corners. That's why I'm trying to keep the adventure playground, because if young people get upset or want to be on their own, they need somewhere to be safe, where the person talking to them is a youth worker saying 'are you OK?', and not a drug dealer saying 'do you want to earn some money?'

For Councillor Hopkins, this requires a different mindset:

> This is a risky business … councillors have to learn to engage
> with the public in a different way, and jump between being an
> intelligence source, an arbiter, an encourager and a decision-
> maker … but the public also has to understand the needs of their
> neighbours; not just representing themselves as individuals, but
> becoming more collaborative across communities. It's messy and
> chaotic, but that's how life is.

PUBLIC-COMMUNITY PARTNERSHIPS

Local government has been changing its role over the past twenty
years, from being a simple provider of services to becoming a
'place shaper' – generating the democratic legitimacy for the
ambitions and endeavours of a whole community. The beginnings of networked government were already emerging at local
level when I wrote about it in 2000, but since then partnerships
have been built and developed, until in most localities partnerships have become the way things are done.[9] Increasingly, other
public organisations accept the legitimacy that the local authority
offers for choosing between social outcomes and setting priorities. At the same time, some local councillors are realising that
their elected role doesn't legitimise them as sole decision-makers.
Their mandate is too frail. But it does give them the legitimacy to
lead a process of discussion and deliberation, bringing different
interest groups together in search of a solution. Some are better at
engaging local businesses, and others better at engaging the
voluntary sector; some are more creative than others. But they all
prefigure a creative mix of public sector, private sector, voluntary
sector and community – a coalition for action that can't be repli-
cated at Westminster.

   When I discussed with him the need to find a balance between
belonging and openness, Robin Murray talked about this new
configuration of public and community action. Politicians from
both right and left have tended to see 'the state' and 'the community' as alternative ways of acting collaboratively. The 'Big

Society' was an attempt by the Cameron government to replace the state with community self-help; while some sections of the left have always preferred state provision to that of the voluntary and third sectors. Robin talks about the 'moat' between the state and civil society. 'It can often feel as if government is a vast castle with protected resources and we the citizens are left on the outside, vulnerable to marauding attackers from the "open economy" unless the state lets down the drawbridge and brings us in to safety'.

He discusses ways to cross the moat: to more closely align the values and behaviour of the state with those in civil society. As he says, each sphere has advantages and disadvantages. The state has legitimate access to vast resources and the power to confront privilege and inequality, but can be bureaucratic and machine-like. Civil society and voluntary sector organisations can be more empathetic, energetic and creative, and bring legitimacy derived from personal investment, relationships and ties to a community, but, because of that local connection, it can be hard for community initiatives to work at the sort of scale that would change outcomes for a whole society, while voluntary groups are not always effective or even sensible. We rely on the state to be fair and prudent, to be honest and honourable, and to conduct public affairs with due process, but we also need the passion, kindness and energy that comes from community-led activity. Citizens collaborate with the government, volunteer, contribute time freely, donate blood and act as unpaid governors of schools and hospitals precisely because we know that no-one is treating the activity as a source of private gain. Reciprocity is a key element of public collaboration: and partnerships depend on it. State organisations often find it hard to work reciprocally, because they are so heavily regulated, and civil society organisations can play a vital role in creating conditions for compromise. At the same time, if state agencies want to work in collaboration with communities they need to unbend and develop a greater capacity for imagination: individuals giving freely want to do so in their own way without too many rules. There is no need to keep these two worlds separate. With wisdom, creativity and generosity on both sides, they can support and learn from each other. They don't have to become the same, they can each contribute to shared projects with different roles.

Robin Murray sees conventional public-private partnerships as diminishing the scope for state action without really offering any alternative legitimacy from which to create new thinking. Much more interesting are public-social partnerships, which create a bridge between the formal legitimacy of the state and the informal, creative energy of communities. He talks about the emergence of co-operative schools, community trusts and open health projects. School hubs can open up the resources of schools to the wider community, and connect up education, health care, social activities and employment. Open healthcare begins with the individual patient, their family and friends and builds health solutions around them, using the resources they already have. There is talk now of creating well-being centres which share resources between mental health trusts and the wider community, using art, dance and fitness to improve health; and community cafes are opening in public buildings as an alternative to Costa or Starbucks.

Projects that bring together public sector and voluntary sector agencies have dual accountabilities, which can create tensions, but, argues Robin, 'these tensions are good tensions, they enable us to create balance – between different collective needs – and create space for a discussion about how to get this balance to work.'

A FOURTH SECTOR?

Indeed we already have a mixed economy of accountability: hybrid organisations – such as Foundation Hospital Trusts, Academies and Community Trusts – have governors accountable to parents, patients or members, while the organisations are regulated on behalf of government. Charities and voluntary organisations that receive public funds are accountable for the spending of that money to government, and for the achievement of their goals to their voluntary boards. Creating the right balance of accountabilities should be the subject of debate and conversation.

Some local authorities, third-sector organisations and community groups are beginning to think about putting together a 'public value' supply chain that involves many different agencies, but keeps resources within the public and community sector instead of being distributed as profit; this would enable combinations of people to own, control and influence what happens. It could be a combination of voluntary organisations, social enterprises, mutuals and health and local government commissioners. It could be a partnership between community trusts and local councils, or a consortium of public sector and community sector providers. The 'circles' that Hilary Cottam talked about in Chapter Five are examples of this. These models are only just emerging, and, sadly, many heroic experiments, including some of the 'circles', are now being starved of funding because of public sector cutbacks. A network of networks could begin to link progressive and creative hospital trusts, housing associations, schools, universities and local authorities with charities, social entrepreneurs and community ventures: creating a supply chain that shares values and agrees collaboratively on social goals, enabling public value to be retained publicly despite the markets within which everyone is operating, so that any profit could be recycled into further social investment.

At a recent Compass event, Uffe Elbaek told us of discussion in Denmark about the emergence of a 'fourth sector' that combines the entrepreneurialism of the private sector and the resources and probity of the state with the creative energy of the voluntary and community sector. He argues that we are only just beginning to experiment with the potential of the fourth sector. His vision of networked and hybrid institutions includes the private sector, but within a new negotiated set of values and accountabilities.

A DIFFERENT SORT OF CONVERSATION

If we are to approach social problems through a 'coalition for action', we need a different sort of conversation within communities.

Conventional bureaucratic process is not creative enough. Across the country, there are experiments in community co-production that go far beyond the conventional consultation exercises and public meetings.[10] Councils are using crowd-sourcing, systems thinking, appreciative enquiry, open space events, world-café techniques and consensus conferences to create a different sort of conversation with citizens.

In an open space event, for example, there is no agenda. People turn up, and the facilitators create space for participants to come forward and suggest the topic for a conversation that they feel is urgent or interesting or important – that brought the out on a cold Tuesday evening. Others suggest other topics. Each topic is written on a large sheet of paper. The participants then choose the conversation they want to take part in. They stay in one conversation or drift into several. When the meeting ends, the actions that follow are those discussed in each conversation. It works.

Barry Quirk, chief executive of Lewisham, has been thinking and writing for many years about how to make local democracy as effective as possible.[11] He is currently advocating a 'civic square' – an arena 'created by public authorities to support comprehensive public dialogue on changes to public infrastructure, public goods, public services and public problems'. The key feature in Barry's vision of a 'civic square' is that no-one is excluded from speaking. It is an arena open to all, including service users, taxpayers, citizens and service providers, businesses, media and elected politicians. What if, instead of making decisions on our behalf, all local authorities saw their role as designing and creating spaces in which communities could come together and decide things collaboratively? Their legitimate role would be to set the rules and tone of the conversation, ensuring all voices are heard, and setting the behaviours that would make the process work. Barry sees this as being backed up by a 'public triangle', a values framework that will test the dialogue through three key questions: what is in the public interest?, how is public value to be realised? how open are public agencies in explaining the reasons for deciding on a course of action?

This is an alternative to the conventional 'stakeholder management' and public consultation with which public bodies are familiar; these, he says, can be manipulated, and are often self-serving, or – constrained by the fear of legal challenge – defensive and over formulaic. Public agencies can only win trust and confidence if they act trustworthily; 'An aspect of trustworthiness is the extent to which public agencies build legitimacy into their actions'.[12] This legitimacy is no longer delivered by experts who decide what is good for us, or by procedural consultation which simply goes through the motions. 'The challenge is to decide "what is right" and that requires deliberation, dialogue and consensus building'. Barry argues that legitimacy comes from including everyone's perspective, and by collectively exploring until we can find a balance between conflicting needs. A combination of deliberative techniques, (community open space conferencing, deliberative polling, citizens' panels and citizens' juries) and 'at large' and direct approaches (referendums, ballot initiatives and so on) can serve to crystallise opinion across different activist groups, civil society and the business community. He wants each public policy decision to have its own 'civic space' – 'in which public agencies engage with everyone in an arena in which all voices are heard and in which different and sometimes competing interests are listened to and heard in a climate of respectful enquiry' (*Civic Square,* p8).

This is a process that helps to explore difference, and find underlying questions and values, one that enables people's ideas to change and grow. Willie Sullivan talked about the value of such a process:

It's not just about setting up a body. It's about the processes of arriving at decisions. There are processes that can lead to almost everyone agreeing – or can lead to those people who disagree recognising the validity of the decision; processes where at the end we say 'well, we've been through this process and we've reached a decision – I might not support it but I've been involved all the way through and so I'm going to go with it'. These ways of working things out could be sophisticated, more involving,

more educative and transformative – which is the most important thing – than just having a vote.

The goal of public dialogue need not be to come up with a
consensus or a shared goal.

In unequal and divided communities that might not be
possible. The tensions might be too great. But by allowing the
conversation to take place, things that are hidden can emerge
into the open. Communities can examine their similarities and
differences. People can learn more about other people and why
they believe what they believe. Understanding could grow. These
could be, in Richard Sennett's terms, dialogic conversations
rather than dialectic ones. Barry Quirk stresses the need to make
sure that public dialogue is open, inclusive and plural, and that
it allows different opinions to emerge and clash peacefully and
creatively.

In my interview with Jeremy Gilbert he talks about the need
for a cosmopolitan ethic or aesthetic in modern crowded cities,
recognising that people come from different traditions, and are
entitled to explain what they believe and why, and argue for their
positions; but also that we need to learn to be tolerant of each
other – accepting difference and plurality. For this to work, we
need agreement about how we work together and how we discuss
and explore – not necessarily agreeing about what we think, or
want, but accepting protocols and procedures for the way we
conduct ourselves. Barry Quirk agrees: 'The overriding need in
the case of public dialogue is for safe, lawful, tolerant and
respectful discussion between people who disagree on public
issues' (*Civic Square, p17*). Purna Sen talks about the importance
of exploring difference:

> We explore difference with respect and we do it without hier-
> archy. We have to learn which differences matter and which
> don't. It would be sad to care about the fact that you wear
> different clothes to me, without seeing that we have the same life
> experiences: whereas wealth, privilege, the ability to have influ-
> ence, they're really significant. But a lot of differences are

horizontal, so they can be dealt with by curiosity. When we discover that we have a different sense of what the world should be like, then that's interesting, that's a starting point for an exploration. We don't get mired in conversations about the differences that don't matter, but we do explore the things we think differently about, and see where that goes.

Chantal Mouffe has called this 'agonistic pluralism'. She argues that thinking about the democratic process as 'leading to consensus and reconciliation' is fraught with dangers, since it assumes that the radical differences in economic interest and world-view and interests can somehow be assumed away. She believes that 'the task for democratic theorists and politicians should be to envisage the creation of a vibrant "agonistic" public sphere of contestation', where people with differing interests and views are not treated as an enemy to be destroyed, but as an adversary whose existence is legitimate and must be tolerated.[13] The future lies in a democracy where we explore difference, learning to understand each other and bringing alternative views into the open, and accept that we must tolerate and live alongside each other. And this has already started – at the edge.

NOTES

1. Harold Jarche, 'Moving to the Edges', Blog post 21.1.14.
2. *The Good Friday Agreement*, Declaration of Support 1998.
3. *Alternativet, The New Danish Open Source Party*, Michael Bauwen P2P Blog.
4. Uffe Elbaek and Neal Lawson, *The Bridge – How the Politics of the Future will link the Vertical to the Horizontal*, Compass/Alternativet 2014, p7.
5. See, for example, NESTA, *Creative Councils; Ten Lessons for Local Authority Innovation*, NESTA, London 2013.
6. See 'Leaders Blog Oldham Council', wordpress.com/tag/jim-mcmahon.
7. Co-operative council toolkit, London Borough of Lambeth.
8. Isabelle Koksal, 'Co-operating with cuts in Lambeth', *Red Pepper*, February 2013.
9. Sue Goss, *Making Local Governance Work*, Palgrave, Basingstoke 2000.

10. See, for example, the Creative Councils experiment sponsored by Nesta and the LGA: www.nesta.org.uk/project/creative-councils.

11. Barry Quirk, *Reimagining Government: Public Leadership and management in challenging times,* Palgrave Macmillan, Basingstoke 2011.

12. Barry Quirk, *The Civic Square and the Public Triangle,* Institute for Government, London 2014, p8.

13. *Chantal Mouffe, Introduction, On the Political,* Routledge, Abingdon 2005.

7. 'WE ARE THE 99%'

So how do we make change happen? Is it worth trying? There seems to be a growing fashion for a 'there's no point trying' cynicism: Russell Brand has been the latest celebrity example. We base our understanding of what's possible on our assumptions about what people are like. Fatalists assume that human nature is fixed, and there's not much we can do to change it, so trying to 'improve' society is pointless: inequality, brutality and suffering are all part of the human condition. Optimists – and socialists have always been optimists – tend to assume that we can make things better, that injustice can be fought, that it is possible to appeal to people's better selves. In the nineteenth century and the first half of the twentieth century, millions of people were inspired to believe that we could create a better society, without poverty, exploitation or hunger – until the cruel totalitarian experiments of the twentieth century shook our belief that such a better society was possible.

Neoliberal thinkers began to crow about 'the end of ideology'. The battle had been won. Fatalists the world over were reinforced in their view that the state can't be trusted to change society. Best leave it alone. But if citizens and the state stop 'interfering', what we are left with is the free market, the unregulated activities of finance capital, and the sinister geek fantasy world of Google. Jeremy Gilbert writes convincingly about the dominance now of a new sort of capitalism, comfortable with social equality and freedom, with open borders and gay marriage, as long as we respond purely as consumers, as long as everything can be bought and sold.[1] Of all the social sciences that emerged in the heady years after the second world war to explain human nature and human civilisation, it is economics that has been accepted in political and popular culture as having the greatest explanatory power; and the assumptions of economics now go almost unchallenged.

Matthew Taylor has popularised Cultural Theory, which proposes that there are four predominant paradigms from which we can view the world – the egalitarian, the hierarchist, the individualist and the fatalist.[2] These perspectives are always in tension – even within individuals. Often we feel torn between egalitarian and fatalist thoughts: we think life could be better, but we can't see any way of changing it, or we are cynical or sceptical about the motives of others. Or we cling to the security of a rule-governed hierarchy but secretly wish for a more bottom-up, empowering, life experience. It is our conversations with ourselves and with each other that tip the balance, build up our courage and enable us to resolve to act – or dissuade us, make us lose our nerve. So what happens in these internal conversations that changes the way we respond?

My interview with Natalie Bennett has been energising and inspirational, because of her refusal to accept that 'this is the way things are'. Spending time with Greens is good for the soul. They are the opposite of fatalists. Greens have always had to be more optimistic than the rest of us – to believe that people will be willing to make personal sacrifices of the comforts of instant consumption, in order to protect the planet. As Natalie reminds me, the world we live in is in no way natural or inevitable. Things are as they are because people created them like that: 'The way things are is because of the actions of government. It's not an accident. We chose to be here, and we can choose to be in a different kind of place'. Natalie talks about reclaiming important values: the values our grandparents learnt in wartime such as thrift, self-reliance, making things last. For Natalie this is an important reminder that our assumptions – about buying things, using things, throwing things away – are recent, short-lived, and could change: 'My grandparents at their diamond wedding anniversary had the same furniture they got married with. They didn't just throw out a good sofa every few years'.

Natalie's eloquence about what needs to change makes me excited, and a bit ashamed about the things we tolerate:

Getting more stuff hasn't made people any happier. Inequality does damage to how we feel and who we are. We need a more equal society, where everyone has the basics – food, comfort, shelter – and we're not trapped, so that we can choose how to live our lives.

She talks about taking back control of our lives:

But we also have to provide this for future generations. We have to go back to one-planet living. We need to restructure our economy. A huge amount of what we do is wasteful – flying empty planes into Heathrow so that airlines can keep their slots! We need to consume less. But we can't simply ask those who don't have enough to eat to cut back. We need a more sustainable economy, a more localised economy, bringing agriculture and production back to Britain, so that we fly fewer goods all around the world to save a few pence. We need goods that are produced without the costs of the damaged lives of child labourers, or of women – like those in Bangladesh – being killed because there was no thought for their safety.

After this interview I sit thinking for a long time. It is easy to dismiss the Greens as having no realistic electoral prospects. But does that mean they are wrong? The values that would enable an open tribe to flourish emerge through my conversations over and over again. I am gaining in confidence that these values might be shared by many, many people. Do I believe things can be changed? Yes. Yes. I know we confront powerful vested interests – unscrupulous and powerful corporate global institutions that like things as they are. We need to ask questions about how real our democracy is. What do we have the power to change? What would happen if we tried?

As Jeremy Gilbert points out in my conversation with him:

The enemy is not markets, or a mixed economy, or competition, or pluralist providers. The enemy is the assumption that the profit motive is the only thing that counts, a world view that turns our whole economy into an individualistic process of exchange.

This world view neither makes sense nor gives us what we need. And it has only been in the ascendency in the UK and Europe for a relatively short time. It was only in the 1980s that we opened up transport, energy, universities, schools and hospitals to market competition and private sector ownership. Now, for the first time since the Thatcher privatisations, there is a debate about whether these changes have yielded any of the gains promised. The privatisation of the railways has cost the public purse more, not less. Renationalisation is now on the agenda, as the East Coast Mainline, temporarily in public ownership, demonstrates how public ownership can make millions for the government. Slowly, questions are being asked about whether the privatisation of the energy and water companies, of the utilities and the infrastructure that enables our economy to function, was such a great idea. It turns out, after all, that state-run services can be just as efficient – if not more so – than privately owned ones, and are more likely to serve the public interest.

There is no inevitable progression towards a totally privatised economy. There are choices to be made. Fatalists argue that people will never vote against their self-interest, but, as we have seen, a narrow preoccupation with personal income isn't really self-interest at all, since the things we most value are our relationships and sense of humanity, the space we have for family and friends, our sense of self-worth and integrity. As Jeremy points out, it wasn't manufacturing, or small businesses, or entrepreneurialism that created the financial crisis. It was a tiny percentage of greedy, unscrupulous bankers. As he says: 'Only 1% of the population gains from this way of thinking. 99% of us would benefit from change'.

Jeremy cheered me up by reminding me that losing the argument is not the same as being wrong. For years, we've been told that there's no turning back, that neoliberal assumptions are now in the public's DNA. But that doesn't seem to be true. Maybe in the early 1980s there was just too much wrong with the dull and bureaucratic state to believe it was capable of working for the people. Maybe the alternatives were not as clear or as good as they are now. Maybe we lacked imagination. I assume that if you've read so far, you are not a fatalist at heart. If you were, you would have abandoned this book long ago. We are not up against an uncontrollable machine or an inexorable system: we are up against unscrupulous, greedy and powerful people. Yes they have a lot of power. So it's going to take a lot to change things. That is why democracy remains such an important element in our politics. In the end, good can win through sheer force of numbers. The constraints are serious. Inertia is a powerful force. But still. Humans are resourceful and energetic creatures. And the new social movements we discussed in Chapter Three may be part of how that resourcefulness creates a different sort of change.

CREATING COURAGE: THE ROLE OF SOCIAL MOVEMENTS

Manuel Castells writes about emerging social movements with the excitement and enthusiasm of a thinker who has been predicting a networked society for many years. Social movements are made up of individuals. Often they start with one person, or with a handful of people, people who show great courage. Social movements grow, because of others who recognise the courage of a colleague or a neighbour and decide to stand beside them. It is this process of standing beside others that changes things. Castells has been documenting the evolution of networked social movements across the globe. He describes the beginning of the uprising in Egypt, when Asmaa Mafhouz, a 26-year-old business student at the university of Cairo posted a Vlog on her Facebook page:

> I, a girl, have posted that I will go down to Tahir Square to stand alone and I'll hold the banner. If you stay home you deserve all that is being done to you ...[3]

Others uploaded the Vlog onto YouTube, it went viral and people began to turn up. History was made. The internet spread the call to action – and some of the most successful networks to spread the news were the fan networks of the Egyptian soccer teams. Of course, in the aftermath, many bad things have happened. But, while the final outcome of the struggles in Egypt is not yet clear, nothing will ever be the same again.

The story in troubled Ukraine is similar. The revolution began when a journalist, Mustafa Nayem, a well-known Ukrainian journalist, posed a question on Facebook after Yanukovych announced he was turning to Russia. Nayem posted, 'was anyone planning to go to the Maidan?' In an hour he got 1000 likes. Four hundred people showed up that night, mostly his friends on Facebook. Then the demonstrations grew, peacefully, at first, until the government snipers began to gun down protestors. Then others took to the streets, the protest changed. It was made up, said Olexiy Haran, a politics professor, of a complex mosaic of people with different motivations, backgrounds and answers, and only turned to violence in outrage against police ferocity.[4]

Castells argues that, for each of us, what moves us from feeling passive, angry but powerless to deciding to act, is an emotional shift. Social movements start with the transformation of emotion into action. And he says that psychologists show that the most relevant emotions are fear and enthusiasm. Fear holds us back – after all, action is risky and uncertain. Things could go terribly wrong. Fear takes us back to the survival instincts that are part of our reptilian brain stem, and the search for comfort comes from our mammalian group instincts. Enthusiasm, on the other hand, derives from hope, and comes from the most recent, the most 'human' part of our brain. Hope is uniquely human, since hope projects behaviour into the future. Hope is an act of imagination. To act, in the face of difficult circumstances, we have to overcome anxiety and fear. And the best, perhaps the only way to do that, is to do it together. Castells says that contact with others builds our courage to act. Our sense of solidarity enables us to overcome fear and to try and change things.

Big changes in society are not made by laws, or by the benign policy-making process of the political establishment. They are made in response to the organised will of the people. If we think back to the major changes in our own society over the past two hundred years – the enfranchisement of working people, votes for women, the abolition of slavery, the reduction of the working week, the end to child labour – they all came about in response to sustained campaigning and mass organisation. 'Social movements are the source of social change and therefore of the constitution of society'.[5]

Social movements can be very powerful. Despite – or perhaps because of – their lack of precision, their location in values and deep emotions – they can topple governments. If hundreds of thousands or millions of people withdraw consent, it is not just democratic governments that fall. The consequences may not be what was intended or predicted. What happens next often depends on the maturity and the wisdom of the established political forces, and/or the judgement and leadership of new ones, and when they fail civil war, or worse, can follow. Of course, change doesn't require the overthrow of governments. Usually it is more gradual, more emergent. The political classes run to catch up, follow the zeitgeist, discover they thought this all along, learn to adapt and change in response to shifting public values. But things change. Old ways, old institutions, old laws collapse, and new ones follow. In time – and time is often a crucial element of emergent change – a new set of solutions are found.

So how might change happen here? Where do we start? What are the tools, the building blocks, with which we might create a different sort of future? From my conversations, four potential building blocks emerged: changing how we make meaning; building a network of networks; creating spaces for enquiry; and remaking social institutions. None of these start with, or depend on, conventional politics.

MAKING MEANING

A first step in change is a change in how we 'make meaning' – how we interpret events, and the values we apply to the actions of others. Through writing, speaking, conversations and symbolic actions, social campaigners are trying to challenge the idea that how things are is somehow a 'natural order'. Castells argues that the new movements he describes are not socialist in any recognisable sense. They often antagonise or oppose the vested interests of left wing and socialist parties and trades unions. Uffe Elbaek refuses to place his new party, Alternativet, in the traditional spectrum from socialist to capitalist. Emerging campaigns are not necessarily anti-business, or anti-commerce; they are about human society being more than just the process of accumulating wealth. They are setting out to change the terms of political debate. The struggle is about how we think, what we assume, and what we take for granted. This is, I think, what Victor Adebowale calls 'the battleground for the human'. As one of the slogans of the Indignados in Spain proclaims – 'we are not merchandise'.

Castells acknowledges that those who have power construct the institutions of society according to their values and interests, but points out too that this process is contested; there is no inevitable result. And while the state can and does sometimes exercise power by violence and coercion, in all societies, and especially in democracies, the use of force requires a degree of consent:

> The construction of meaning in people's minds is a more decisive and more stable source of power. The way people think determines the fates of the institutions, norms and values on which society is organised.

Willie Sullivan talks about how this is exactly what is happening in Scotland. Through the work of Common Weal, Compass and others, the idea of what Scotland is and can be is opening up. The terms of the conversation are changing. The network is beginning to generate a shared language:

> The idea of the commonweal is beginning to make sense to people. Commonweal is an old word that means the commonwealth: all this stuff belongs to us collectively but is not being used in the interests of all of us collectively, some people are getting a lot more out of it. So they have been looking at different kinds of propositions. We've had a politics of 'me first'. We've bought into an idea that if we look after ourselves then we'll do better. But it's been proved wrong. A 'me first' politics means all

of us last, whereas an 'all of us first' politics is more inviting and seems more plausible.

The way people think is created through communication, through conversation, through talking and writing. Until recently that communication was dominated by a few powerful people and organisations, newspapers, commercial interests, government, television channels, but, because of the internet and social media, the control of meaning is opening up. In Scotland, the media is different from the media in England. It is more local and more connected to Scottish experience:

> There's a different kind of media, and while I'm not sure that in Scotland the population is more democratic or left-wing, the opinion formers and commentators – the 5% who make opinion – are more willing to put forward alternative views. Since devolution these are the people who have moved into positions of influence. And while we still look towards Westminster, the political arguments and debates are shifting away to our own culture, and our own opinion formers are coming more to the fore.

As Castells argues, power is exercised by 'the construction of meaning in people's minds'. And where there is power there is also counter power: the capacity of social actions and movements to challenge the power that is embedded in institutions. At a time like now – when in many countries there is widespread disaffection with the established political institutions, and a sense that 'no-one can hear us' – there is scope for others to begin to define values and actions in new ways. The future forms of our institutions and our culture depends on the outcomes of these struggles. There is everything to play for.

A NETWORK OF NETWORKS

A second potential source of change is a new sense of connectivity across civil society. In the UK there is a plethora of charities, think-tanks, pressure groups, organisations and campaigns – not only the older and more established ones, but new arrivals such as 38 Degrees, UK Uncut, Locality, and Transition Towns. Websites such as More Like People, Corporate Rebels, Mumsnet, The People Who Share and Thoughtworks are changing how we work together.

Social movements work in different ways from conventional political parties. They are, by definition, loose networks rather than organisations. Sometimes there is a formal organisation at the core, but many of the newer organisations are experimenting with a new, more open 'belonging', which doesn't require membership or subscriptions. Many people act and get involved, without always knowing precisely what they believe, but wanting to draw attention to something, to express something. Social movements are about values and beliefs. They are always about imagination. By their very nature, they capture people's energy and enthusiasm, and people choose to put their energy into many different issues and causes. Each has a network and a group of supporters and activists. Each has its own approach. This can be fragmented and confusing – too many different projects and movements – but the plethora of movements and campaigns can create new stories, and show how we could live by different values.

What is perhaps new is a willingness of social movements to connect and to learn from each other. We are seeing the beginnings of a 'network of networks' – where people with very different concerns come together to see what they have in common. Instead of the factionalism and in-fighting of the 1970s, we are seeing movements recognising each other's contribution and valuing each other's strengths. Journalists and commentators are not being pressurised to 'take sides' in sectional battles, they are acknowledged as contributors of ideas. In Scotland, whatever happens in the referendum, this process seems to be fruitful and creative. Willie Sullivan talks about a new opportunity opening up:

Because of this opportunity comes a willingness to work together. I don't know if it comes from the left experiencing so many defeats by doing things in the old way – trying to get everyone to join one organisation, arguing that everyone else's organisation is wrong. That approach has been tried and failed so often. But now there seem to be an understanding that one organisation can't do everything, and that different organisations do different things better. I think it comes from a growing confidence, and a security in what we believe. People are beginning to realise that open networks are the way that things work: so why wouldn't you do it like that? And I guess that's been facilitated by technology and just getting to know and understand each other a little bit more. For example, we are learning that the Radical Independence Campaign can mobilise lots of people, while Common Weal have the ideas and the evidence and the papers. And Compass Scotland has been able to support them, and say that Commonweal has the ideas, we don't want to claim everything for Compass. And now our ideas are feeding into their work and vice versa.

Carys Afoko talks about similar thinking in the rest of the UK:

So, for example, Compass should connect more with organisations like 38 Degrees, organisations that are new and fresh and come from a different set of origins. They've got two million people on their email list, so they can get a large number of people to engage in a deep way, while Compass can get a smaller number of people to engage in a deeper way. We can we link up with them and get them more deeply involved, make them feel welcome ... encourage them to set up a local group or stand for Parliament. We should be finding the people who are already doing things well and helping them to do it, finding out what else we can do, using the strengths of different groups. Compass is good at getting ideas out there, but who is good at reaching out to people who have never been involved before? Who is good at mobilising outside London – in the North, or the West?

A combination of virtual connectivity and face-to-face conversations can begin to build a loosely connected set of movements across civil society, able to exchange and transmit new ideas, perhaps capable of acting together if they chose.

CREATING SPACES FOR SOCIAL ENQUIRY

If we want to rethink the assumptions of our society, we need a space in which to do it. If we are to make progress on the dilemmas of advanced capitalist democracies, we need to move beyond old rhetoric and what Jon Cruddas called 'the fixed solution', to create new social processes of solution-finding. If official politics is reduced to the sound-bite and the script, then within civil society we need to strengthen the capacity for citizens to learn about the world around them, to balance conflicting stories, to make judgements.

Rosie Rogers says:

> People need to do a lot of soul searching and think about what they want to believe and what they want to see happen. For example, if Labour truly cared about democracy, they need to blast open their policy review, get on the bus, have picnics in the park, and ask people what they think. They need to listen and not be scared of what's going to come back.

Jon Cruddas talks about needing to create not 'multi-cultural spaces but inter-cultural spaces where people come together'.

The living wage enquiry, sponsored by the Joseph Rowntree Foundation, led by the Bishop of York, is one example of a 'citizen enquiry': it was not ordered by government, not dominated by the establishment, but brought together academic, philanthropic, campaigning and civil society organisations to investigate an issue of huge social importance. It did not wait for government; it moved ahead of politicians.

Castells talks about 'reconstructing the public sphere in the spaces of autonomy, built around the interaction between local places and internet networks ... finding ways for humans to manage collectively their lives according to principles that are largely shared in their minds and usually disregarded in their everyday experience'.

For political old-timers, experiments in participative democracy and assembly-based decision-making will no doubt lead to a deep sigh and a sense of déjà vu. Jeremy Gilbert said: 'we need more meetings, the more complex the society the more participation you need' – but the idea of more meetings makes most of use shiver. But that is, in part, because of the sorts of meetings we have become used to. We are turned off politics because there is nothing more infantilising than being lectured from a podium by a middle-aged man reading a speech that someone else wrote. But a discussion about important things with people who think deeply but differently is exciting. Open space, appreciative enquiry, simulations – these enable people to have serious conversations which lead to something, instead of being lectured to in large halls. Why don't we use these techniques more? Designed well, a large scale conversation about what sort of society we should have would be fascinating, joyful; it would change the way we think about ourselves and others. The technology that enables these conversations is getting more sophisticated, but, really, it isn't difficult. All that is needed is politeness, generosity and a passionate interest in other people.

We could find ways of doing politics that are not closed, forbidding, elitist and only available to the entitled political classes. We need a politics that is welcoming, warm, inviting. Compass's Change How (un)conference in 2013 was just such an event – 500 people involved in open space discussions, with mindfulness and relaxation sessions, comedians, food, adventure – and at least half of the attendees had never been to anything 'political' before. People brought their mums, or their kids. The sense of being in a vast room full of people who were open-minded, curious, generous and willing to change was inspiring. We need more political events that make us happy.

RETHINKING SOCIAL INSTITUTIONS

Robin Murray talked about old 'closed' institutions that struggle with the new open world. What would social institutions look like if they were redesigned with imagination to balance our human need for belonging with recognition of the need for openness? If we don't want every part of our lives to be dominated entirely by

Google and Apple, we need good social institutions. Social institutions define what is important other than cash exchange. They are the manifestation of the slogan 'we are not merchandise'. They offer spaces where people come together from different backgrounds and beliefs, where our common humanity outweighs our wealth or our religion or our accent. Crucially, they are the places where the rules of engagement for civil society are constructed; where the cultural assumptions and norms are created. If we are to find Victor Adebowale's emphasis on a society capable of 'love, wisdom and respect', we will look for evidence in the quality of our social institutions.

Social institutions face choices about the role they play in society, choices about whether to simply compete and survive within the political context in which they find themselves, or to join in a process of redefining that context. We tend to treat institutions such as hospital trusts, universities, arts organisations, etc, on an either-or basis: either they are simply run by the government, or they are run purely to make money. But in governance terms neither of these pictures is true. Of course they are constrained by regulation or by lack of public funding, and of course they fare best when an entrepreneurial spirit and ambition drives them; but they are also hybrid organisations, possible precursors of a fourth sector. We have yet to fully explore the potential this offers for change. Our social institutions have yet to create a shared self-consciousness about the power, and the responsibility that this hybrid status opens up. The role of lay governors and community representatives as well as non-executives in social institutions is under-valued and under-explored. There is scope to create radical governance models and user-led organisations; to experiment with ways to engage and involve service users at every stage in a school, a university, a hospital trust, a community trust, a housing association, and to experiment with mutual and social ownership forms. The best social institutions are 'making meaning' by defining their values and intervening in the public and political debates that shape their world, and standing up for right against wrong. It can take courage to challenge ministers and regulators, or to attempt to reshape markets based on social value, but there are thousands of public and third sector organisations doing so. But, despite the plethora of organisations representing each social sector, we have not yet fully explored the scope to create 'a network of networks' between sectors. Could our social institutions work together to redesign and rethink their role?

Such organisations could have a role, too, in creating social spaces for citizen enquiry, through offering their facilities and resources and leading new thinking. Some are already doing this. The National Housing Federation is leading thinking about the future of housing; the Joseph Rowntree Foundation sponsors social enquiry. But could universities, instead of simply turning themselves into education supermarkets, join together to frame a debate about the sort of education that would equip people to live in open tribes? Could hospital trusts, Clinical Commissioning Groups, clinical colleges and the Royal College of Nurses work together to imagine a more human and empathetic health system? Could sports and leisure organisations challenge our work-life balance, and arts organisations lead a conversation about 'the unexamined life'? We need new social institutions to participate in conversations outside their specialist areas, to help shape thinking through the clash of cultures and the spark of difference.

THE ROLE OF THE MEDIA

New media are opening up all the time. We are daily discovering new sites – blogs and tweets and web-based journals as well as conventional media (Though it should be noted that finding our own way in cyberspace can be time-consuming and frustrating: there is a lot of nonsense out there; and in cyber-space women can be subject to extreme abuse simply for expressing an opinion.) We depend on print journalism, television and radio not least for their ability to curate the unlimited supply of 'stuff' and focus our attention on what matters. And in spite of the nastiness of much of what passes for journalism, there are still honourable and serious newspapers taking their role as investigators seriously.

But we should ask more of all journalism and broadcasting, using mechanisms for public accountability and consultation where they exist, and challenging the values that underpin the decisions they make. The media create the conditions for enquiry. Fearless investigative journalism pays a role in this. But there are more complex issues, such as how elections are reported: if they are simply treated as sports fixtures between opposing teams, the political process is further devalued. And simply being neutral between Westminster political parties is not enough in a world where nearly half the population have stopped voting. Media organisations with social values have to help us explore alternative versions of how society could be. (Sometimes, occasionally, a Radio 4 lecture or a BBC programme does this – though often in a timid, conventional way, and for an elite audience.)

The license fee is important because it enables the BBC to operate in a way that supports the public interest and develops the public sphere, in ways that would be difficult for a commercial service. But it also makes the BBC risk-averse and over-responsive to government. The BBC is still, arguably, the single most powerful and important social institution in the UK. Rather than allow it to be driven into either becoming another commercial provider, or the tool of government, we should be strengthening its independence and asking more of its role in reinforcing and creating the social values that underpin our democracy. Channel 4 and other third sector media organisations could play a similar role. If we want to create space for the transmission and exchange of ideas, we need to move beyond simply asking for 'public service broadcasting', and begin to ask that they champion social enquiry.

Why do we never see public consultation or collaborative problem solving on TV? With so many reality TV shows, why not bring together citizens' juries to consider social problems and find new solutions? If the deliberations of a jury are exciting enough for a best-selling play such as *Twelve Angry Men*, why could they not be the basis of a TV show? Why do we treat poor people as a spectator sport in *Benefits Street*, rather than engaging with and understanding their experience and perspectives? If people enjoy watching reality TV programmes depicting community projects to rebuild someone's home, why do we not also have programmes based on community projects to tackle youth unemployment or solve community tensions? Why don't we ever hear about the community circles that Hilary Cottam talked about, or about co-operatively owned old people's homes? We get *The Choir*, with its famous and charismatic leader, but we don't celebrate the leadership and the courage of local people. Public service broadcasting is not simply about content, it is about style and tone. It is about moving beyond compliance and survival. If the resources and creativity that are aimed at drama and lifestyle programmes were used to design engagement with the questions that dominate our political future, could we create exciting television from a process of collaborative enquiry?

THE VERTICAL AND THE HORIZONTAL

Castells argues that social movements cannot help but concern themselves with the democratic process:

> Because if citizens do not have the ways and means of their self-government, the best designed policies, the most sophisticated strategies, the best-wished programmes may be ineffective or perverted in their implementation. The instrument determines the function. Only a democratic policy can ensure an economy that works as if people mattered, and a society at the service of human values and the pursuit of personal happiness.

Given the widespread contemporary debate about the failure of conventional politics, what could link these ideas to our current political parties? Is the disconnect now so wide that a solution via conventional political parties is no longer imaginable? If all three parties think the same, and none of it reflects what most citizens experience and feel, is the social response limited either to apathy or a vote for UKIP? Or is there the potential here for a grass-roots politics that emerges from civil society and works entirely differently? How do we challenge the underlying values that are seen in conventional politics? Indra Adnan writes about a change that happens when you are not looking – a 'soft powered world' that deploys 'the tools of engagement, connection and influence more successfully than arms, money and clout'.[6]

Until recently the main connection between centralised political parties and the wider public has been the constituency, the locality. Lisa Nandy talks about the value of this, and the need to protect the representative role in constituencies:

When people who are rooted in their community come to Westminster, different issues come into the agenda. Too often the debates that we have in Westminster are dictated by a small group of people who live in London and who have quite privileged lives. We don't talk enough about the things that people talk about in Wigan. I'm accountable, and can't walk down the street in Wigan without people coming up to me to tell me what they think.

So for some, the strength of that link to place is how the vertical connects to the horizontal. But locality isn't the only way we group ourselves and create a sense of tribe. As we explored in Chapter One, shared projects and values are also important in creating solidarity. But the mainstream political parties have drifted a long way away from their origins in values-led organisations, and are increasingly distant from the vast array of values-based organisations that could help bridge the gap – charities, faith communities, campaigning groups, NGOs and pressure groups. Private sector lobby companies and global corporates have a much clearer route to decision-makers than most social and civic organisations.

And it can be hard to make links. Movements like UK Uncut and Occupy don't have programmes or clear demands. They are about values and ideas, or seek to raise the profile of a problem or a question. Conventional politicians dismiss this sort of politics as unfocused and lazy. And it is true, as John Harris argues, that without the resources and the power that the state holds it is impossible to challenge powerful vested interests: 'You have to be able to capture the state … you can't redistribute income sitting in a tent outside St Pauls'.[7] But something important is nevertheless being said here, and points to the limitations of conventional politics. Jeremy Gilbert summarises the dilemma between conventional party politics and social movements:

> Do we need a vertical response, a well-disciplined organisation, a return to effective party politics and a restoration of traditional community values? Or a horizontal response, a rejection of a discredited political system, new forms of networked organisations and a break from all forms of hierarchy and institutions?[8]

His answer is that we need both. Good politics needs effective institutions, but it also needs an experimental dimension, working to break down concentrations of power wherever they arise. The situation would be improved if political parties could begin see themselves again as loose alliances, connecting a wider set of social movements into Westminster; having a core membership but also a far wider group of active supporters. They could turn outwards, and see their constituency not as their shrinking membership but as a network of networks, connected into many localities and to many causes. Politics would then become a process of 'negotiation and renegotiation, of shifting alliances and coalitions building the capacity and the platforms for the most equal and participatory forms of engagement possible – places where we can share and collaborate'.[9]

A DIFFERENT APPROACH TO GOVERNMENT?

If we had a different sort of politics, we might have a different approach to government. Not only political parties, but also Whitehall departments, could become more open and accessible.

Government departments could recognise the role of other bodies in bringing ideas together and building solutions. Instead of academics, intellectuals, NGOs and charities having to fight their way into a policy-making process that is dominated by consultants and lobbyists, they would be there at the beginning: forming the problems to be investigated, and contributing ideas throughout the process. The policy process could move away from the current obsession with short-term initiatives of a kind that ministers can badge and deliver during their brief tenure of office.

A longer-term view of how we might solve social and economic problems could engage the expertise and experience of wider civil society, and encourage politicians to work across party lines.

In the light of the kinds of solutions emerging at local level that we discussed in Chapter Six, the control of local provision through centralised government departments becomes increasingly problematic. Whitehall mandarins find it very difficult to work on a cross-boundary basis, and – trained as they are to see accountability to 'their' minister as 'trumping' all other sorts, and despite the difficulties caused by the absence of the legitimacy that would arise from the active commitment of others – nothing changes. The prize must be to bring the resources and expertise of many different organisations to bear on very real and practical problems. How do we support mental health within a community? How does a school use its resources to support education among adults as well as children? Robin Murray spoke of a transition in the way global corporations are organised, away from departments and towards projects, and I explored similar ideas in my chapter in a book entitled *After Blair*.[10] These ideas raise wider questions about how Whitehall itself could become part of a public-community collaboration. How would the civil service organise itself if this were to become a possibility? In practical terms, as Robin and I discussed, it might mean government projects working in the way a film unit works: the people who need to come together to achieve a certain outcome do so, and at the end they go their separate ways into other, different projects, but with the experience of having worked together and the memory of a success – of having belonged to a kind of temporary tribe.

So perhaps we could begin to think about a very different sort of state, one that connects out into civil society, not necessarily to control it, but to put public resources behind it, in ways that could even out difference and ensure life chances, in support of innovation and creativity. Let's not get carried away. Bureaucracy and inertia will always haunt government organisations; politicians will always worry about risk; and big organisations will always move frustratingly slowly. But still. Maybe a shift is possible.

The democratic spaces needed to sustain an open tribe are hard to imagine at Westminster. But even Westminster would begin to change if politicians behaved differently. The more people do that, the more the stereotype will change. When will we learn to trust MPs? When they become trustworthy. And that will mean saying what they truly believe, and sharing with us the complexity of their deepest thinking, their doubts and their dilemmas.

None of this is easy. The defensive behaviours that Carys Afoko and Rosie Rogers talk about so eloquently in Chapter Three will not easily change. We have a long way to go before mainstream political parties become open and curious, before young women, or black and Asian politicians, feel welcome, before politicians listen rather than make speeches. Politics is always about who we are and what we value, how we behave, who we listen to, and the assumptions we make. But new things are being felt, and said.

Willie Sullivan talks about a new generosity. There are still egos, of course, but there's a greater awareness of the need to suppress egos, the need to work together. It's a kind of confidence thing. It's about trust'. Carys Afoko says:

> It involves a different way of linking up between movements. It means you don't have to agree – we can accept that you're not going to like everything I say and I'm not going to like everything you say. You're going to have to change yourself to get on with me and I'm going to have to change myself to get on with you. I don't have to like every group in civil society. Some of them might want to do things that are naïve or stupid. But we don't have to be purists. If we want to build something bigger, we have to see where we can agree – but there's also an issue about generosity, instead of competiveness.

At the Change Now (un)conference, the final plenary discussion was about how we could become respectful and kind, not to allies but to political opponents. Could we treat the arguments of those who are attacking us as serious and interesting? Could we approach our adversaries with curiosity and appreciation? Neal Lawson and Uffe Elbaek argue that nowadays being a rebel involves 'being kind'.[11] Can we create a culture in which kindness is not considered weak? In which power is exercised through a willingness to listen, rather than talk? In which the skills needed to become a politician are entirely different? There are already examples of MPs and Lords challenging the conventional wisdom of what politics is supposed to be like. But without help they will be defeated, or will leave.

Politicians, as much as any of us, need to become everything they are capable of being: to draw on their full humanity, experience and wisdom; to experiment and sometimes fail; to be able to admit their failures. Could we help them to feel more, laugh more? Be less afraid? We already have good examples of politicians – for example Jon Cruddas, Lisa Nandy, Natalie Bennett and Stella Creasy. The conversations I had with MPs and members of the House of Lords were often very funny, creative and open – not at all like the interviews we are used to seeing on the news. We need to keep the boundaries open between social movements and conventional politics, to see what might emerge.

NOTES

1. Jeremy Gilbert, 'How does change happen and how do we make it?', Compass post, 18.11.13.
2. Cultural Theory was originated by Mary Douglas, and has been refined by a number of thinkers and recently popularised by Mathew Taylor. See, for example, Matthew Taylor, 'The Search for Clumsy Solutions', *Guardian*, 1.10.09; or his RSA blog.
3. Manuel Castells, *Networks of Outrage and Hope: Social Movements in the Internet Age*, Polity Press, London 2012.
4. *Guardian*, 14.03.14.
5. Castells, *Networks of Outrage and Hope*.
6. Indra Adnan, 'In New Times change happens while you are not looking', Compass website, 18.11.13.
7. John Harris, quoted in Elbaek and Lawson, *The Bridge*, p7.
8. Jeremy Gilbert, 'How does change happen'.
9. Elbaek and Lawson, *The Bridge*, p6.
10. Sue Goss, 'Re-imagining the Public Realm', in Gerry Hassan (ed), *After Blair: Politics after the New Labour Decade*, Lawrence and Wishart 2007.
11. *The Bridge*, p6.

CONCLUSIONS

I started this project to try out a different way of conducting an enquiry into politics. So, just over a year on, what has this series of conversations taught me?

It has taught me that the quality of talk matters. In a good conversation something is built, something is made. We often see interviews on the news and in documentaries in which nothing new happens. I begin to see that this is not because there are not exciting things waiting to be said, but because of the process of the interview, the nature of the questions, the contextual assumptions – all these cut off the supply of real talk. Too often the dominant media create artificial, dull and meaningless conversations. Les Back argues that we need to challenge the style of contemporary public dialogue, shaped as it is in British culture by adversarial, gladiatorial programmes such as Question Time, and character- ised by self-confident, aggressive speakers determined to tell you the answer:

> Our culture is one that speaks rather than listens. From reality
> TV to political rallies, there is a clamour to be heard, to narrate
> and gain attention. Consumed and exposed by turns, reality is
> reduced to revelation and voyeurism.[1]

In conventional politics, dialogue is reduced to waiting for one's turn to speak. In most television interviews, a pack of experts or politicians have to battle for one or two minutes of airtime in which to deliver pre-prepared messages.

I have learned to value the good question better than the slick answer. I had moments of joy when my interviewee said some- thing unexpected, something which broke through a blockage, something that made me almost gasp with the new thought that poured through. One of the radical things we can do is to begin to talk differently together, to ask open questions, to explore difference with respect and curiosity. The best question I asked was of David Marquand. In discussing why it was not a programme or a manifesto we needed, he said, 'It would be more like throwing a pebble into a pond and watching the ripples'. I thought for a moment and asked, 'What would the pebble be?' – and that led to a fascinating discussion which still resonates with me.

I have begun to firm up my thinking about the sort of political activity that will make sense over the coming months and years. I have taken part in debates about the future of political parties. And I have started to think that – though our current parties may change, or different parties may emerge – Westminster doesn't seem to be the most important political space just now. While I was cooking dinner a few months ago I listened to a debate between Paul Mason and Manuel Castells on Radio 4. Mason argued that all this horizontal stuff was fine as far as it went, but change needed powerful leaders. Castells replied with the patience of an academic who has studied social movements for fifty years: 'change will come'. Systems, he said, can only evolve peacefully when they internalise the social tensions and something new emerges, institutions are eroded, new public opinion is created; eventually this translates into new voting patterns. If that is so, then the need now is to create spaces outside parliament where different conversations can be had, where we might explore the social and democratic institutions of the future; where different communities, different age groups, different political parties, different causes might come together. Compass has begun to work in this way, and, for everyone participating, this is changing us. There is an important project to find the social resources to make these spaces available, and bring them alive.

I have been thinking about networks. I'm not a social media person, but I am beginning, slowly, to find the networks of likeminded people from whom I can gain sustenance and energy. However it seems to me that, while ideas can be floated on the web, if we are to bring thinking to a conclusion, if we are to act on what we think, we need to meet up. Somehow the connectivity between events where people come together, and a wider web-based conversation, is beginning. My interviews pointed to the many social movements and campaigns blossoming at the expense of formal politics – and the growing networks between these groups. These are no longer about narrowly 'political' issues: there is an urgency about exploring how to live our lives, what matters, relationships, marriage, friendship, parents – not since the 1970s has there been so much talk about how to 'be'. There has always been some element of 'counter-culture' in social movements, but this time we need to make sure the conversations include the young, the disconnected, and ordinary families who don't yet believe that what they think and feel is relevant to politics.

I have been struck by the importance of a politics of generosity at a time when we are being told to close up, to shut down, to defend ourselves against immigrants and outsiders, to narrow down who we see as being 'like us'. This isn't just about the language we use and the messages we transmit; it is about finding ways to continue to feel open, curious, confident, hospitable, generous. A politics of generosity is one that explores ideas happily, and doesn't seek to close down arguments or vilify those who think differently. It treats everyone's views with respect, and helps to identify what we disagree about with precision, so that we can enquire more deeply. It is about not feeling threatened by ideas that we don't agree with, but instead treating them as starting points for exploration.

Of course, the entirely legitimate criticism of this book is that I have chosen for my conversations people with whom I agree. And while this is partly true, I didn't know whether we would agree when I started, and sometimes I have changed my views as a result of what I have heard. It is part of the paradox I'm exploring that we tend to explore our ideas within relatively safe and comfortable spaces before we are willing to expose them to strangers.

Nevertheless, I can see how important is the next step – beginning discomforting conversations with people who think very differently. Perhaps that is another book.

I have, of course, begun to think about the implications of the idea of the open tribe for our personal lives, as well as for social organisation. Have we got the balance right between our tribalism – our sense of belonging, connection and solidarity – and the growth that comes from learning, change, dislocation, adventure? Have I? I have been left wondering about many things: while this book is completed, the thinking is not.

I have been thinking also about my own work-life balance and sources of meaning. If we want to change things, then we probably need to put into practice a determination to show and celebrate sources of meaning other than work and consumption. In the most hard-hit parts of Europe people are beginning to create an alternative economic culture, in response to the meaninglessness of a consumer-based life when you no longer have the money to consume. They are developing barter networks, social currencies and co-operatives. I already work for an employee-owned mutual, and know how that intensifies the values and the passion I and colleagues put into our work. But I have asked myself what is, really and truly, the most important thing in my life? So I have been thinking about the campaign of Anna Coote and others to achieve a shorter working week. What would an economy built on love be like? Actually, I realise, many of the most important people in my life are already living in this way: already living on a pension or as a full-time carer, or earning not very much doing something they love dearly – poetry-writing, academic studies, gardening, aromatherapy, designing websites, making jewellery. How could we begin to celebrate this – to treat the workaholic as someone with a problem, begin to scale down the stuff we need?

My conversations also gave me courage. All these wise people, dedicating their lives to making things better, in some cases looking back over fifty or sixty years of endeavour, have never given up, are still as passionate as they ever were; their dreams are still as strong. I have been thinking about what it means to become fully human. It seems to me that this is a choice we can make in our lives, what-ever the constraints and difficulties – although this may be at a greater cost for some than for others. It takes courage. All the people I have interviewed have in important ways shown courage. They have put their values into action. They have found the energy to do new things, to invent, to create.

Finally, I have been struck by the absence of anxiety in all the people I spoke to. Many writers have talked about the good life in terms of emotions and values, intimacy, wisdom, creativity, love. But there is an element of the good life which is not about having things, or even about successful relationships with others, but is about the absence of anxiety. That doesn't come from lives that are trouble-free, but from a feeling that we have power over our lives, are able to influence events, able to take action, if need be, in accordance with our values. If we don't have the society we want to have, we need to act, together, to find it.

NOTES

1. L. Back, *The Art of Listening*, Berry 2007.

Biographies of main interviewees

Victor Adebowale CBE is Chief Executive of the social care enterprise Turning Point and was one of the first to become a People's Peer.

Carys Afoko is advisor to Lisa Nandy MP and previously worked at the New Economics Foundation.

Natalie Bennett is an Australian politician and the leader of the Green Party in England and Wales.

Hilary Cottam is a design strategist, social entrepreneur and founder of Participle and Relational Welfare.

Jon Cruddas is Labour MP for Dagenham and Rainham and head of Labour's Policy Review.

Janet Daby is a Labour councillor in the London Borough of Lewisham and cabinet member for community safety.

Jack Hopkins is a Labour councillor in the London Borough of Lambeth and cabinet member for safer and stronger communities.

Jeremy Gilbert is Professor of Cultural and Political Theory at the University of East London and editor of the journal *New Formations*.

Francesca Klug, OBE, is a professorial research fellow at the LSE in the Centre for the Study of Human Rights and Director of the

Human Rights Project. Formerly she was independent academic advisor to the government on the model for human rights.

Ruth Lister, CBE, is a member of the House of Lords and Emeritus Professor of Social Policy at Loughborough University, and an academic and campaigner on poverty.

David Marquand is a political writer and historian, a former Labour MP, and Principal of Mansfield College (Oxford University).

Robin Murray is an industrial economist, and has been a fellow at the Institute of Development Studies at the University of Sussex, a co-founder of Fair Trade organisations and of the environmental partnership Ecologika, and a fellow of the Young Foundation.

Lisa Nandy is MP for Wigan, and entered the House of Commons in 2010. She is Shadow Minister for Civil Society.

Rosie Rogers is National Co-ordinator for Compass, and an active member of UK Uncut and UK Uncut Legal Action.

Purna Sen is Labour candidate for Brighton Pavilion and Deputy Director of the Institute of Public Affairs. She was formerly Head of Human Rights in the Commonwealth Secretariat.

Willie Sullivan works as the Scottish Director of the Electoral Reform Society. He is a founder member of Compass UK and the convenor of Compass in Scotland.

Lee Waters is Director of the Institute of Welsh Affairs, and a former chief political correspondent for ITV Wales and BBC producer.

Sue Goss is a writer and a political scientist, and works as an individual and team coach, and as a systems leadership and strategic advisor to public and third sector organisations.